Same-Sex Marriage

— AND —

American Constitutionalism

Same-Sex Marriage

— AND —

American Constitutionalism

*A Study in Federalism, Separation of Powers,
and Individual Rights*

MURRAY DRY

PAUL DRY BOOKS
Philadelphia 2017

First Paul Dry Books Edition, 2017

Paul Dry Books, Inc.
Philadelphia, Pennsylvania
www.pauldrybooks.com

Copyright © 2017 Murray Dry

Printed in the United States of America

*To Cecelia, my loving wife
and mother of our children,
Rachel and Judith*

Contents

CHAPTER ONE

An Introduction

THE TWO DECADES LONG CONTROVERSY OVER SAME-SEX MAR-
riage in the United States was finally resolved on June 26, 2015, when
the U.S. Supreme Court handed down a 5-to-4 decision in *Obergefell
v. Hodges*, which held that the Fourteenth Amendment's Due Process and Equal Protection Clauses required states to allow same-sex
couples to marry on the same terms as opposite-sex couples.[1] Justice Kennedy wrote the court opinion, joined by Justices Ginsburg,
Breyer, Sotomayor, and Kagan. Chief Justice Roberts and Justices
Scalia, Thomas, and Alito each wrote separate dissents.

Justice Kennedy began his opinion with a broad claim, reminis-
cent of John Stuart Mill's *On Liberty*, which he then linked to the
issue in the case.

> The Constitution promises liberty to all within its reach, a liberty
> that includes certain specific rights that allow persons, within a
> lawful realm, to define and express their identity. The petition-
> ers in these cases seek to find that liberty by marrying someone
> of the same-sex and having their marriages deemed lawful on the
> same terms and conditions as marriages between persons of the
> opposite sex.[2]

When Justice Kennedy turned to the Constitution's Due Process
Clause and to Supreme Court decisions concerning an unenumer-
ated right to privacy and a fundamental right to marry, he signaled
his approach with another broad statement:

The nature of injustice is that we may not always see it in our own times. The generations that wrote and ratified the Bill of Rights and the Fourteenth Amendment did not presume to know the extent of freedom in all of its dimensions, and so they entrusted to future generations a charter protecting the right of all persons to enjoy liberty as we learn its meaning. When new insight reveals discord between the Constitution's central protections and a received legal stricture, a claim to liberty must be addressed.[3]

While Justice Kennedy acknowledged that the Court's marriage cases "presumed a relationship among opposite-sex partners," and that the Court had summarily rejected a challenge to Minnesota's traditional marriage law in 1972,[4] he presented four principles to explain why analysis of the right to marry decisions "compel the conclusion that same-sex couples may exercise the right to marry."[5]

1. ". . . the right to personal choice regarding marriage is inherent in the concept of individual autonomy."
2. "the right to marry is fundamental because it supports a two-person union unlike any other in its importance to the committed individuals."
3. "[the right to marry] safeguards children and families and thus draws meaning from related rights of child-rearing, procreation, and education." In this connection, Justice Kennedy noted: "hundreds of thousands of children are presently being raised by [same-sex] couples."
4. "marriage is a keystone of our social order."[6]

After describing the many benefits that accrue to the status of marriage, Justice Kennedy concluded: "exclusion from that status has the effect of teaching that gays and lesbians are unequal in important respects. It demeans gays and lesbians for the State to lock them out of a central institution of the Nation's society." Therefore:

The limitation of marriage to opposite-sex couples may long have seemed natural and just, but its inconsistency with the central meaning of the fundamental right to marry is now manifest. With that knowledge must come the recognition that laws excluding same-sex couples from the marriage right impose stigma and injury of the kind prohibited by our basic charter.[7]

The dissenting justices asserted that the Court had veered from a judicial determination of what the law *is*, to a policy determination, which is rightfully the province of legislatures, of what the law *should* be. Chief Justice Roberts wrote:

> Petitioners make strong arguments rooted in social policy and considerations of fairness. . . . That position has undeniable appeal; over the past six years, voters and legislators in eleven states and the District of Columbia have revised their laws to allow marriage between two people of the same sex.
>
> But this Court is not a legislature. Whether same-sex marriage is a good idea should be of no concern to us. Under the Constitution, judges have power to say what the law is, not what it should be.[8]

For the dissenting justices, because the traditional understanding of marriage involved the union of a man and a woman for the sake of procreation and effective child-rearing, preventing same-sex couples from marrying could not be termed discrimination against homosexuals. While the understanding of homosexuality had changed (it was no longer thought to be an illness by the medical profession), and while the attitudes of many homosexual couples toward marriage and child-rearing had changed, their exclusion from the institution of marriage did not violate anyone's fundamental rights.

Perhaps more than any other recent political and legal controversy in the United States, this one involves what the noted constitutional scholar Philip Kurland identified as the "three elements" of the American Constitution: the republican form of government, which includes federalism; the separation of powers, in particular the division between the popularly responsible political branches and the popularly insulated judiciary; and the importance of individual rights, which is mainly how Americans understand their liberty and hence what they expect their government to protect.[9]

In this book, I examine the debate over same-sex marriage from two different if overlapping perspectives, which can be called the moral-political and the constitutional, respectively. The first refers to the question: which policy is best and hence should be adopted by those bodies, legislatures normally, charged with making such decisions. The second refers to the limitations that the American Constitution and the institution of judicial review impose on such legislative, or directly popular, decisions. Those decisions must work within the legal limitations imposed by our fundamental law, as interpreted by judges, finally by the U.S. Supreme Court.[10] This book is as much about the separation of powers, in particular, judicial review, as it is about same-sex marriage, because I think the controversy over the latter topic reflects a dangerous tendency to regard judicial power as no different in kind from political power. When the requirements of constitutionality approach the requirements of wisdom, by which I mean the best policy, we run the risk of displacing self-government in America onto the courts and the nomination and confirmation process for judges.

Most advocates of same-sex marriage regard legislatures and courts as alternative institutional means of achieving their end, to be selected on the basis of what is most likely to succeed. Opponents of same-sex marriage fear the consequences of fully legitimating same-sex unions by permitting same-sex marriage, and yet they have difficulty making this argument persuasively, partly because it seems to reflect hostility to homosexuals generally and partly because they support governmental objectives that restrict what freely consenting adults wish to do. Increasingly, American courts have interpreted the Constitution to put the burden on advocates of such restrictions, by, for example, requiring them to demonstrate that the resulting conduct would result in clear harm.[11] This is something that opponents of same-sex marriage were unable to do. That does not necessarily mean that no harm would result, only that it might take a number of years to determine what, if any, effect same-sex marriage would have on the institution of marriage and, in particular, the children raised by same-sex couples.

Our constitutional separation of powers reflects a significant difference between legislative and judicial power; members of Congress are subject to periodic popular elections, Article III judges are appointed for life. I acknowledge that interpreting an eighteenth-century Constitution, with critical amendments that were passed and ratified nearly one hundred and fifty years ago, requires an appreciation of the need for interpretation. To paraphrase Chief Justice John Marshall, expounding a constitution is not the same as interpreting a prolix legal code.[12] In conformity with the distinction between legislative and judicial power, Publius' separation of powers argument in Federalist 47 and 51 differs from his separation of powers argument in Federalist 78. The former two essays concern the checks and balances resulting from an overlapping of the governmental powers of the two houses of Congress and the president. The latter essay concerns the need for insulating the judges from electoral responsibility, so that they will have the fortitude to uphold the Constitution, even against legislative abuses.[13] I take this to mean that the framers did not regard the judiciary as simply another political branch of government.

The lively controversy over same-sex marriage provides me with a perfect opportunity to demonstrate the sometimes subtle but important differences between political and judicial power. That is because while I think there are enough good reasons to support same-sex marriage as a matter of policy, I also think the argument for retaining traditional marriage has enough substance that it should not have been judicially invalidated, either on the grounds that it reflects homophobia or on the grounds that it lacks any "rational basis."[14]

While it is perfectly understandable that supporters of same-sex marriage look to the end and do not care whether they achieve their objective in the courts or through legislative action, it should matter to American citizens how significant laws and practices are changed. What is at stake is preserving an adequate space for republican government to flourish. In a different constitutional context, the one that involves the relationship between the two Religion Clauses in the First Amendment, the Supreme Court has twice advocated the importance of allowing a "play in the joints."[15] In that context, the Court referred to allowing either Congress or state legislatures some discretion with respect to an accommodation between the demands of the Free Exercise Clause and those of the Establishment Clause. I think that something analogous applies in other constitutional contexts, including the controversy over same-sex marriage. The courts should not always press legislatures to make what the courts regard as the best choice in a conflict between governmental authority and individual rights. Notwithstanding the Court's decision in this case, some "play in the joints" is necessary to allow popularly elected legislatures to make some important choices. There are several reasons to support such an approach.

For one thing, those who do not support same-sex marriage, whether from hostility to homosexuals or from an attachment to traditional views on marriage, are much more likely to accept a legislative decision against their preferences than a judicial one. Furthermore, if the courts were not so willing to be in the forefront of political and constitutional change, opponents would be less likely to turn to constitutional amendments as the means to attain their objectives. That too takes the issue out of the ordinary political process. Courts have developed doctrines for examining issues that involve either individual rights and/or classifications of individuals that have the effect of increasing the range of judicial power at the expense of political power. I refer to the now commonly accepted three levels of scrutiny, with the two "heightened" levels requiring an almost perfect fit between the end sought and the means chosen.[16] It is noteworthy that the Court did not follow the suggestion of the Government and hold that classification by sexual orientation must be subject to heightened scrutiny. Moreover, while the Court treated the case in terms of the fundamental right to marry, it made no reference to the application of strict scrutiny. Of course, its argument on behalf of autonomous choice and dignity seems to have produced the same result. I return to this theme in chapter two.

The court opinion's emphasis on the extent to which the subject had been considered does not fully acknowledge the extent to which courts, first state and then federal, took the lead in bringing about this significant change in marriage law in the United States.

SAME-SEX MARRIAGE HAS been under active consideration in American government since 1993,[17] when the Hawaii Supreme Court held that the state's marriage law, which did not allow same-sex marriage, would be subject to strict scrutiny[18] and would likely be found invalid. That prompted Congress to pass the federal Defense of Marriage Act (DOMA), in 1996, which both guaranteed that each state was free to determine its own marriage laws (section 2) on the one hand, and defined marriage as the union of a man and a woman for the purposes of federal government benefits (section 3) on the other.[19]

Hawaii did not introduce same-sex marriage, but in 2003 the Supreme Judicial Court of Massachusetts held that its state constitution required same-sex marriage. Moreover, from 1993 to 2009, the highest court in each of the following states decided a same-sex marriage case: Hawaii, Vermont, Massachusetts, New York, Washington, New Jersey, Maryland, California, Connecticut, Iowa. Five state high courts either were poised to decide (HI) or decided in favor of same-sex marriage (MA, CA, CT, IA), and five state courts either upheld the state's traditional marriage law (NY, WA, MD) or required equal benefits but not marriage (VT, NJ). The highest court in the District of Columbia denied the same-sex marriage claim in a brief per curiam opinion.[20] Then, on April 7, 2009, the same day that Vermont's legislature voted to allow same-sex marriage, the District of Columbia's city council voted unanimously to recognize same-sex marriages. And on June 24, 2009 New York, through legislative action, joined Massachusetts, Connecticut, Iowa, Vermont, New Hampshire (which had also acted legislatively) and the District of Columbia in allowing same-sex marriage. After President Obama announced, in a television interview on May 9, 2012, that he supported same-sex marriage, and with public polling showing that a majority of the American people favored same-sex marriage, the following states enacted laws authorizing same-sex marriage: Washington (November 6, 2012); Maine (November 6, 2012); Maryland (November 6, 2013); Rhode Island (May 2, 2013); Delaware (May 7, 2013); Minnesota (May 14, 2013) Hawaii (November 13, 2013), and Illinois (November 20, 2013).[21]

Moreover, in December 2010, Congress repealed Don't Ask, Don't Tell legislation that prohibited homosexuals in the military from acknowledging their sexual orientation.[22]

The same-sex marriage issue became a federal case in 2009, when same-sex couples in California went to federal district court to challenge the constitutionality of that state's Proposition 8, a constitutional referendum which overturned the effect of the California Supreme Court's decision holding that its constitution required that same-sex couples be allowed to marry. Plaintiffs won in the district court[23] and in the Ninth Circuit Court of Appeals.[24] Then, on the final day of its 2012 Term, the Supreme Court decided that the supporters of Proposition 8 did not have standing, either in the Supreme Court or the court of appeals, to appeal the district court's decision; this left the district court's decision, which applied only to California.[25] On the same day, the Supreme Court, in *United States v. Windsor*,[26] affirmed the lower federal court decisions striking down section 3 of the federal Defense of Marriage Act, which had defined marriage for federal (benefit) purposes as the union of a man and a woman. As a result of that decision, a superior court judge in New Jersey ruled that since the state supreme court's decision in 2006 held that the state's constitution guaranteed all rights and benefits of marriage to same-sex couples, and since those rights now included federal benefits, the state had to allow same-sex couples to marry.[27] Shortly thereafter, the New Mexico Supreme Court held that its constitution required same-sex marriage.[28]

More significantly, according to a report from Lamba Legal, from the Court's *Windsor* decision to the day before the decision in *Obergefell* was announced, there were "49 rulings in 48 cases from 30 different federal courts invalidating or fully or partially enjoining enforcement of the marriage bans of 29 states and the territory of Guam." In addition, there were "17 rulings in 17 cases from 15 different state courts totally or partially invalidating the marriage bans of 7 states . . . bringing the totals to 66 rulings in 62 cases from 45 different federal and state courts invaliding or enjoining the enforcement of the marriage bans of 32 states and the territory of Guam since *Windsor*."[29]

After the U.S. Courts of Appeals for the Fourth, Seventh, Ninth, and Tenth Circuits affirmed the unconstitutionality of such bans, the Court of Appeals for the Sixth Circuit, by a vote of 2-to-1, reversed the rulings of district courts in four states, upholding bans on same-sex marriage. That led to the Supreme Court's decision, on January 16, 2015, to accept the case for review.

That the controversy over same-sex marriage was heated and engaged the partisans on both sides was due, in part, to the hostility to homosexuality that derived from some religious teachings stemming from Biblical passages, in the Old and the New Testaments, condemning such behavior. While American government officials swear to uphold the Constitution and not the Bible, and the Constitution contains a prohibition on religious tests for office as well as two First Amendment clauses supporting religious liberty, religion nonetheless plays a prominent role in American politics. Tocqueville observed in *Democracy in America*: "Religion, which, among Americans, never mixes directly in the government of society, should therefore be considered as the first of their political institutions; for it does not give them the taste for freedom, it singularly facilitates their use of it."[30] Some might say that religion mixes too much in American politics today and that the opposition to same-sex marriage exemplifies the problem. I return to this contention in my concluding chapter.

To provide the proper context for this controversy, I begin, in chapter two, with our constitutional framework. The most important part of this framework involves the separation of powers, in particular that aspect of it which recognizes that the judiciary stands apart from the legislative and executive branches of government in having a special responsibility to say what the law is, rather than to make it or to execute it. I think that the same-sex marriage controversy exemplifies the benefits and the drawbacks of judicial review in American government today. Unlike other works on the subject,[31] this book will examine the controversy first in terms of its moral and political merits and then in terms of constitutional arguments. My intention is to support a form of judicial review that recognizes the place of legislatures, as well as the importance of rights, in American democracy. The same-sex marriage controversy is a good subject for this point because I think the case for same-sex marriage is right in terms of policy, or wisdom, but traditional marriage laws should nonetheless have been upheld as constitutional.

A second aspect of the constitutional framework is federalism: we are a nation of states and the federal government is a government of enumerated powers. Moreover, and this has become increasingly important in American government, the highest courts in the several states have the final authority to interpret their states' constitutions, as long as those interpretations do not violate any federal authority, which is supreme within its sphere.[32]

To illustrate the difference between the question "What should be done?" and the question "Is it constitutional?" I treat each question separately. In chapter three, I consider the moral and political arguments for and against same-sex marriage. Then I turn to the judicial consideration of the topic. I first treat U.S. Supreme Court decisions bearing on the topic indirectly: these include equal protection and due process cases that have given rise to an increased judicial scrutiny of legislation in matters concerning race, sex, and privacy. In the next chapter I examine the judicial decisions in those states where the highest[33] state court handed down a decision on a same-sex marriage claim. Then I turn back to the federal courts in chapter six. I examine the first federal case, initially *Perry v. Schwarzenegger*, which became *Hollingsworth v. Perry* on appeal, from the district court to the Ninth Circuit and then to the Supreme Court. I then examine *Windsor*. Finally, I take a look at federal court decisions since these two Supreme Court decisions and I return to the Supreme Court's decision in *Obergefell*. I then conclude with an explanation for how I understand the same-sex marriage issue and why I think the Supreme Court should have resolved to leave the matter in the political process.

CHAPTER TWO

The Supreme Court in the American System of Government

Separation of Powers and Federalism

A. The Separation of Powers and Judicial Review

THE SUPREME COURT'S DECISION ON SAME-SEX MARRIAGE, LIKE other recent controversial decisions,[1] may produce attacks on judicial review and on life tenure for Article III judges. In this chapter, I want to defend judicial review and life tenure for our Article III judges. I offer my own understanding of judicial review and relate it to the views of other constitutional scholars who have written on the subject. This kind of inquiry is sometimes presented in terms of judicial activism versus judicial restraint. A related formulation contrasts "textualism" or "originalism," referring to the plain meaning of the Constitution and/or the understanding of the framers, with a contemporary understanding, also referred to as a "living constitution approach."[2] Another important formulation contrasts legal formalism with legal realism. Legal formalists emphasize the difference between legislating and judging, or between law making and law finding; legal realists regard the formalist distinction as a fiction. That is because they emphasize the inherent gaps, or indeterminacy, in the law. This is true of the Constitution. Many parts describe general principles that require thoughtful application to issues and circumstances that the framers and the ratifiers of the Constitution could not have been aware of and hence did not consider. As a result, legal realism goes together with "the living constitution," and virtually "everyone is a legal realist now."[3] The view that I wish to present takes issue with that formulation while accepting the insight that judges often "legislate" when they apply general principles to particular cases; this is especially true when they follow common law reasoning, which respects precedent but often reinterprets precedent to reflect doctrinal developments. I agree with the realist insight that there is not always a clear distinction between legislating and judging, between making policy and applying law in particular cases. But the constitutional forms suggest that judges need to be aware of the importance of popularly supported legislative deliberation and choice. In contrast to some formalists, who appear to hold the positivist view that whatever cannot be logically demonstrated is a mere preference, or "value judgment,"[4] which for that very reason must be left to the legislature, I think judges need to consider the rational basis of laws seriously, or "with bite," as Gerald Gunther coined the phrase.[5] If they find a genuine rational basis for a law, they should uphold it, even if they think the stronger argument lies on the other side. In the subsequent chapters, I make the case for the constitutionality of traditional marriage laws, while acknowledging the stronger argument for allowing same-sex couples to marry, and then I critically examine the state and federal courts' treatment of the issue.

The Founders' Constitution and Judicial Review

In the first volume of *Democracy in America* (1835), Alexis de Tocqueville wrote: "there is almost no political question in the United States that is not resolved sooner or later into a judicial question."[6] That is because political questions can usually be presented in terms of rights claims, which can be related to constitutional provisions and hence made subject to judicial authority.

Judicial power has often been controversial. In *Marbury v. Madison*,[7] Chief Justice Marshall drew on Alexander Hamilton's argument in Federalist 78 to hold that the Supreme Court had the power to invalidate an act of Congress contrary to the Constitution. He argued that the peculiar province of the judiciary is to say what the law is and that the Constitution is the supreme law in the United States. But as president, Thomas Jefferson, who first assumed the courts would exercise judicial review and urged James Madison to support a bill of rights for that reason (which he did), later argued in favor of each branch of government's having the final authority over that part of the Constitution that addresses it.[8] Of course, it is not always clear that a given legal question comes under the province of only one department. In *Marbury*, Jefferson and Marshall disagreed over which branch had final responsibility for deciding when an appointment had been made.

Another alternative to the Hamilton-Marshall position was offered by state Supreme Court Justice John Gibson in the Pennsylvania case of *Eakin v. Raub*.[9] According to Gibson, judicial oversight of Congressional acts stopped at making sure that the constitutional forms were followed: that the bill had been passed by both Houses and signed by the President or that both Houses passed the bill by the required two-thirds if the President vetoed the bill. Judge Gibson's proposal has not been adopted, although Justice Felix Frankfurter attempted to introduce a version of this approach when he argued that apportionment was a "non-judiciable political question."[10] The Supreme Court decided otherwise in *Baker v. Carr*.[11] In 1993, however, the Court held that the Impeachment Clauses, which vest the "sole power" to "impeach" in the House and the "sole power" to "try" in the Senate, were non-justiciable.[12] This could be called a limited version of the Jefferson-Gibson "departmental" approach to interpreting the Constitution.

The Supreme Court's decision in a case involving the Constitution does not necessarily settle the matter, even leaving constitutional amendment aside. When the Court struck down the Missouri Compromise in *Dred Scott v. Sandford*[13] in 1857, Abraham Lincoln, whose entire Republican Party platform was based on a restoration of the Missouri Compromise, claimed that he could accept the decision in the particular case of Dred Scott without having to accept the decision as a binding precedent for the future.[14] If so, he claimed, that would take the very important question of Congressional power under the territorial government clause out of the hands of the political process, of Congress and the President.[15] Lincoln's argument was implicitly accepted when he won the presidency in 1860 on a platform of moral opposition to slavery and hence political opposition to the extension of slavery into the territories. Lincoln did acknowledge that after a certain time, and number of cases, a decision must be accepted as binding precedent. Judicial review, then, is consistent with each department of government having a constitutional responsibility.

Two Critics of Judicial Review

In *Packing the Court: The Rise of Judicial Power and the Coming Crisis of the Supreme Court*, the late political scientist James MacGregor Burns argued that "judicial review," which he puts in quotes, is nothing but "a judicial veto . . . of legislation," and that "[t]he framers did not include a judicial veto in the Constitution *because they did not want it*."[16] According to Burns, Marshall's *Marbury* opinion was "a brilliant political coup" which "declared that it was the exclusive duty of the Supreme Court, not Congress and not the President— to say what the law is."[17] Marshall did not say, nor did Hamilton, on whom he drew, that it was the "exclusive" duty of the Supreme Court to say what the law is, only that it was their "peculiar province." The actual formulation is not inconsistent with Lincoln's later insistence on the difference between deciding a particular case and establishing a rule that the other branches must follow.

Equating judicial review, so understood, with judicial supremacy, Burns concluded his book by urging opposition to "a hostile court repeatedly striking down vital progressive legislation"[18] and by proclaiming "John Marshall was wrong: it is emphatically the province and duty of the American people, not the nine justices of the U. S. Supreme Court, to say what the Constitution is."[19]

Larry D. Kramer has offered a more nuanced argument in his book, *The People Themselves: Popular Constitutionalism and Judicial Review.* Professor Kramer argues that Americans of the eighteenth century distinguished between fundamental, or constitutional, law and regular law and that while the courts had the final say over ordinary law the people had the ultimate say in matters of constitutional law. Because the Constitution was "the people's charter," "it was 'the people themselves'—working through and responding to their agents in the government—who were responsible for seeing that it was properly interpreted and implemented. The idea of turning this responsibility over to the judges was simply unthinkable."[20] For Kramer, that accountability took the form of periodic elections, the right of petition, trial by jury, where the jury is free to decide questions of law as well as fact, and, in the extreme case, mob rule, or "mobbing."[21] As Kramer interprets the precedents, including state court decisions in the 1780s, "judicial review was not an act of ordinary legal interpretation. It was a political—perhaps we should say a 'political-legal'—act of resistance."[22]

But the notion that the judiciary interprets the Constitution as law and acts on behalf of the people is consistent with the development of the doctrine of judicial review as we know it. Hamilton made precisely that claim in Federalist 78, and the Anti-Federalist Brutus assumed that the Supreme Court would have the final power to interpret the Constitution, as a result of the "arising under" clause in Article III ("The judicial power shall extend to all cases, in law and equity, arising under this constitution.").[23] Hamilton's argument, in Federalist 78, was that the Constitution was supreme law due to its popular mode of ratification, a point that Madison made in the Federal Convention. Then, Hamilton added that the courts act for the people because "the interpretation of the laws is the proper and peculiar province of the courts."[24] All governmental power, on the framers' view of government, comes from the people, but the people do not directly exercise governmental power, no matter how important popular elections are; they elect those who act for them, save in the extreme condition when they conclude that the established government needs to be altered or abolished. Kramer essentially tries to constitutionalize Locke's discussion, to which he refers, of the people's ultimate authority to place and displace government; only for Locke this authority is a "pre-political" power that precedes government and when called into being amounts to a "dissolution" of government, also known as revolution.[25]

There is an alternative to Hamilton's argument, and Jefferson offered it in his proposal for a state constitution for Virginia in 1783. He suggested that constitutional controversies be submitted to the people through a convention whenever two-thirds of two branches proposed one. Yet, as Kramer pointed out, Madison criticized this proposal in Federalist 49, where he wrote in support of tradition. Because most human beings are attached to what is familiar to them, Madison thought that those attachments, which he called "the prejudices of the community," should be on the side of the government. For that reason, a people's constitution should not be easily amended.[26]

Kramer's proposed popular constitutionalism has the effect of bringing the people into government in precisely those difficult cases where the different departments of government disagree. Allowing the people to place and displace their governors periodically is different from allowing them to decide the tough issues of government directly. The framers, and Madison in particular, thought that one task was more appropriate for the people than the other; that is why there is no provision for popular referenda in the Constitution.[27]

When the framers discussed their expectations for judicial power in the Federal Convention, they disagreed over whether the judiciary should be joined to the executive branch in the veto over acts of Congress, but they assumed that the judges would pass on a law's constitutionality in the course of adjudication. And no distinction was made between judicial interpretation of statutes and judicial interpretation of the Constitution. Kramer quotes a key speech of James Wilson, who, along with Madison, supported the council of revision, a body of judges along with the executive who would have a veto over legislation. Both Madison and Wilson feared that the executive would not have enough popular support to sustain such a check on the legislature. Wilson went so far, in the passage Kramer quotes, to argue that while in fact "the judges, as expositors of the laws, would have an opportunity of defending their constitutional rights" in court, more was needed. "Laws may be unjust, may be unwise, may be dangerous, may be destructive; and yet may not be so unconstitutional as to justify the Judges in refusing to give them effect."[28] Wilson's argument makes explicit what I think was commonly accepted by the framers: that a judicial determination of what the law requires, even law in the form of a constitution, differs from a political determination of what laws should be passed. Wilson's remarks thus anticipate Justice Frankfurter's distinction between constitutionality and wisdom, which becomes the basis of an argument for judicial self-restraint.

Elbridge Gerry opposed joining judges with the executive in the veto. He also made a very striking statement in light of the current controversy over judicial power. After objecting to what he regarded as an improper mixing of powers, especially because the judges as members of the council of revision might have a second look at the same law as judges, Gerry said: "It was making Statesmen of the Judges; and setting them up as the guardians of the Rights of the people. He relied for his part on the Representatives of the people as the guardians of their Rights and interests."[29]

In some way Gerry supports Kramer's argument, in so far as Kramer opposes the extent of power that judges now exercise. But Gerry was arguing against giving the judges a legislative veto, in contrast to a judicial power to interpret the laws in relation to the Constitution. One might say that as judicial power has developed, and generally become accepted, what Gerry feared from the council of revision has occurred with judicial review, and by and large the people accept it and approve of it. But, as we have seen, resistance develops as the Supreme Court invalidates legislative acts involving controversial public policy.[30]

Kramer maintains that while some framers discussed judicial review and assumed that the Supreme Court would interpret laws in light of the Constitution, most framers did not discuss the matter because "Judicial review was not the question before the Convention. The question was how best to prevent the enactment of unwise and unconstitutional federal legislative measures. The answer was an executive veto."[31]

Granted that that was the framers' focus, I think Kramer's interpretation plays down the significance of the language of the Constitution, as well as the explicit, albeit limited, discussion of judicial power. By the language of the Constitution I refer not only to the Supremacy Clause, which does, as Kramer points out, assert federal supremacy as against state laws, but also the beginning of Article III, section 2: "The judicial power shall extend to all cases in law and equity arising under this Constitution, the Laws of the United States, and Treaties, made or which shall be made, under their Authority; . . . ."

Chief Justice Marshall's argument for judicial review in *Marbury v. Madison* drew on this language, as Hamilton had in Federalist 78. There Hamilton defended the life tenure of Article III judges by saying that political independence was necessary to allow the judiciary "to declare all acts contrary to the manifest tenor of the Constitution void."[32] He gave as examples clear prohibitions on legislative power, from Article I, section 9. And the Anti-Federalist Brutus drew on the very same language to predict, albeit with alarm, the importance of judicial power.[33]

Once the Court affirms the power to invalidate an act of Congress inconsistent with the Constitution, and once that practice becomes accepted by the people, it is not easy to prevent judicial review from becoming judicial supremacy.

Kramer discusses numerous writings of Madison to argue that the "Father of the Constitution" denied any special authority in the courts to interpret the Constitution until late in his life, in 1834, when he affirmed that "It is the judicial department in which questions of constitutionality, as well as of legality, generally find their ultimate discussion and operative decision: and the public deference to and confidence in the judgment of the body are peculiarly inspired by the qualities implied in its members. . . ."[34] Kramer regards this position as irreconcilable with Madison's earlier statements, in the Federalist, the Virginia Report, and the First Congress, to the effect that all departments of government, federal and state, had a responsibility to preserve constitutional limits of government.[35] But all that means is that the people have ultimate control of government through periodic elections, constitutional amendments, and, ultimately, the right to alter or abolish governments that fail to secure the people's rights. Even in the most controversial case of his states' rights argument, in the Virginia Resolutions and the Virginia Report, Madison limited himself to communicating with the people in the other states with a view toward expressing opposition to the Alien and Sedition Acts. This ultimately resulted in Republican Party victories in the 1800 elections. This would have allowed the representatives of the people to rescind the Alien and Sedition Acts, but that was not even necessary since the laws terminated on March 4, 1801.

Madison must have realized that constitutional interpretation worked better with judicial decisions than with any suggestion that the people themselves could invalidate judicial decisions by something like a constitutional referendum. Madison the constitutionalist may well have supported actions of "We the People," in the form of informed consent and elections, but he did not support direct popular participation in government. That is clear from his powerful argument in support of the extended sphere, in Federalist 10, as well as his argument in support of what he called modern representation, in which the people did not exercise political power in their collective capacity, in Federalist 63.[36]

The burden of Kramer's argument is that when the Supreme Court assumes that it has an exclusive responsibility to say what the Constitution means, as it did in the Little Rock desegregation case,[37] and again in a more recent commerce clause case,[38] the people have surrendered their ultimate authority to govern themselves. He explains his position this way: "Bear in mind that popular constitutionalism never denied courts the power of judicial review: it denied only that judges had final say."[39] Were we starting from scratch,

Kramer would favor the approach of Western European countries: the establishment of a special court to adjudicate constitutional issues and to have its members elected for a fixed term by an extraordinary majority. That would limit the effect of the finality of judicial decisions. Since he does not think such a constitutional amendment is likely to pass, Kramer suggests various ways in which the people, employing Congress or litigation, can attempt to rein in the Supreme Court.[40] His object is to cause the Justices ("though the analogy is more suggestive than literal") "to see themselves in relation to the public somewhat as lower court judges now see themselves in relation to the Court: responsible for interpreting the Constitution according to their best judgment, but with an awareness that there is a higher authority out there with power to overturn their decisions—an actual authority, too, not some abstract 'people' who spoke once, two hundred years ago and then disappeared."[41]

Kramer identifies this position with Madisonian republicanism. And yet, as active as Madison was in addressing legislatures, state and federal, about constitutional matters, he made a point of praising American representation over that found in ancient Greek and Roman democracies on the ground that the former is characterized by "the total exclusion of the people, in their collective capacity, from any share in [government]."[42] And that is precisely why the people, in their collective capacity, do not have constitutional authority over the Supreme Court.

NOTWITHSTANDING THAT, I agree with Kramer that Supreme Court pronouncements about their having exclusive or even final authority over the Constitution, beyond the particular case, is false and potentially harmful, if it causes the people to defer to the Court without thinking about the issues themselves and without expecting members of Congress to do so either. On the other hand, it's difficult to support such opposition without also encouraging what Kramer called "mobbing," a mass disobedience of a legal decision.

I do not know what Kramer would say about the Court's recent same-sex marriage decision. On the one hand, it surely goes beyond invalidating laws that were "contrary to the manifest tenor of the Constitution." On the other hand, by the time the Court handed down its decision in *Obergefell*, public opinion polls supported gay marriage, even though only twelve states had gotten to that result via the political process.

Other Controversies over Judicial Review

I turn now from challenges to judicial review in its entirety or to judicial supremacy as Kramer describes it to controversies about how courts should interpret the Constitution. One disagreement pits "originalism," which refers to the framers' understanding of the text of the Constitution, versus "the living Constitution," which emphasizes the need for a contemporary understanding to reflect evolving standards of justice. Judge Robert Bork and Justice Scalia are associated with the former position; Justice Brennan is associated with the latter.[43] Neither position is fully satisfactory. The originalists, unlike the framers whom they claim to follow, are skeptical of any argument from principles of natural justice; they regard such arguments as expressions of "value judgments,"[44] meaning mere preferences. Perhaps as a result, they try to limit general language to the most concrete practices accepted at the time of ratification.[45] In some cases, they find a way to reconcile originalism with an opinion that everyone now supports (*Brown v. Board of Education*) or they may support a doctrine (a robust view of freedom of speech) on the grounds of stare decisis, but without a reconsideration of their overall approach.[46]

Advocates of the "living constitution" approach, on the other hand, are sometimes willing to ignore the clear meaning of constitutional language if it implies an outcome they oppose. Justice Brennan, for example, continued to vote against the death penalty even after a number of state legislatures amended their capital punishment statutes to comport with the Supreme Court's requirements, and notwithstanding the reference to capital cases in the Constitution itself.[47]

Jack Balkin attempts to reconcile these two positions with what he calls "Living Originalism." Professor Balkin distinguishes "the ascertainment of meaning" from "constitutional construction." By giving originalism more breathing room, Balkin can then empha- size construction, "implementing and applying the Constitution using . . . arguments from history, structure, ethos, consequences, and precedent."[48] This differs from Justice Scalia's originalism by not being limited to "original expected application."[49] Balkin ar- gues that his theory is more consistent with American constitu- tional development, because "political and social movements and post-enactment history shape our constitutional traditions."[50] He also emphasizes the role of "We the People" in contradistinction to the courts, as the most important determiners of how the Constitu- tion is to be construed.[51] The originalists are concerned about the undue scope for judicial power that the "living Constitution" posi- tion provides. Balkin's response appears to be twofold: first, in prac- tice judges are constrained by many sources, including judicial and non-judicial precedents, and, as he later adds, their mode of appoint- ment; and second, a theory of constitutional construction "should start with interpretation by citizens as the standard case," view "in- terpretation by judges as a special case," and expect all branches of government to engage in constitutional construction.[52]

Balkin emphasizes the development of the principle of equality in American constitutionalism, with reference to the New Deal and the Civil Rights Revolution.[53] He describes the related increase in classifications subject to more than rational basis scrutiny, and while his discussion of the civil rights of homosexuals is limited, his prin- ciples would seem to support judicial invalidation of traditional mar- riage laws.[54]

Balkin does a good job of showing how a basic governmental framework can continue to instruct and constrain government offi- cials, while language reflecting standards or principles can be sub- ject to changing construction. In one of his summary chapters, Balkin refers to the New Deal and the civil rights revolution as he takes issue with Alexander Bickel's formulation of judicial review as having to surmount the "counter-majoritarian difficulty."[55] Balkin's response is that "judicial review is integrated into democratic processes and does not stand fully outside them."[56] He is satisfied that there are enough constraints on the Supreme Court, as a result of the appointment process, legal standards, professional culture, etc. that there is no need for concern about judicial review trumping democratic constitutionalism. As evidence of a "bipartisan" concern about judicial review, Balkin cites the recent homosexual sodomy and gun rights cases; both were decided by 5-to-4 votes and both produced cries of judicial activism. Interestingly, Balkin proposes a form of "court packing" to encourage more senior justices to retire, in order to produce more "rotation" on the Court.[57]

Balkin's argument never explicitly addresses the question of how judicial power is different from legislative power, and what that means for judges when they are confronted with constitutional questions. I think Balkin would say that he covered the difference in his discussion of legal precedents and standards of legal reasoning. Courts have to write opinions justifying their decisions, and that requires treating both text and precedent as that material is presented by opposing counsel. But there is no further recognition of the difference between a law that is constitutionally permissible, even if not the most desirable, and another law that is not constitutionally permissible. In other words, Balkin's constitutionalism accepts the legal realist's contention that there is no workable, conceptual distinction between lawmaking and law finding.

In this respect, Balkin's argument reminds me of Judge Richard Posner's argument for a pragmatic approach to judging. When Judge Posner defends his pragmatic approach to judging in response to an argument from democratic accountability, he argues, drawing on Aristotle, that American government is a mixed regime and the judiciary is an oligarchic part.[58] But American government is not simply an Aristotelian "mixed regime." Modern democracy, which employs representation to gain the security that the "extended sphere" provides, also relies on the non-Aristotelian categorization of governmental powers into legislative, executive, and judicial. Because the foundation of American government is a popularly elected legislature, judicial power, in the form of final decisions by judges appointed for life terms, must be exercised with caution if popular or self-government is to be maintained.

For legal realists, how a judge draws the line between the constitutional and the unconstitutional seems to depend on preferences that cannot be reasoned about, plus a disposition either to intervene or to hold back. If nothing else, the Constitution's Founders, who knew what they were doing when they established Article III courts with life tenure, were not legal realists. Otherwise they would not have constructed offices that had life tenure.

The position I am advocating starts from the Founders' position on the judiciary and the possibility of distinguishing the constitutional question, as one of legal permissibility, and the policy question, as one of practical wisdom. I think Balkin is right to insist on a combination of "originalism" and the "living constitution" approach, for that is the only way to respect the text of the Constitution and make it work for American government today. A strict originalism would necessitate periodic amendments, if not a second Constitutional Convention. But by reading into the Constitution a strong commitment to equality and by minimizing the difference between judicial action and consent of the governed through elected legislatures, Balkin's Living Originalism supports a substantial judicial participation in the political process.

B. Federalism and Same-Sex Marriage

America is a nation of states. The most common manifestations of this are separate state governments and equal state representation in the U.S. Senate. Vermont has as many senators as California. As important as the several states are for American government, the federal government's legislative powers are substantial; beyond the extensive enumerated powers, Congress may also "make all laws which shall be necessary and proper for carrying into execution the foregoing powers, and all other powers vested by this Constitution in the United States."[59] In addition, the framers adopted a Supremacy Clause to establish the superiority of federal over state authority.[60]

While a civil war was necessary to defeat secession, federal supremacy has rarely been challenged since.[61] But the principle of federal supremacy is compatible with separate and diverse constitutional decisions by state supreme courts, if those decisions are based on an "adequate and independent state ground" and do not implicate any federal right.[62] At the urging of Justice Brennan in the 1970s,[63] state supreme courts began to base some of their decisions exclusively on their own state constitutions. If these decisions recognized rights not recognized by the Supreme Court, they would stand unchallenged as the state courts had the final say on the meaning of that state's constitution. At this point, we see the intersection of the separation of powers and federalism in the same-sex marriage controversy. Advocates of same-sex marriage, when unable to attain their objective through their state's legislature, turned to the courts. In addition, these advocates, anticipating that they would lose in the federal courts, and especially in the Supreme Court, fashioned their constitutional arguments in state courts exclusively on state constitutional grounds.[64]

In 1993, the Hawaii Supreme Court ruled that the state law limiting marriage to opposite-sex couples was a sex-based classification presumably in violation of the state's Equal Protection Clause. The court remanded the case to the lower court with instructions that it consider whether the state could justify its traditional marriage law under what is known as the "strict scrutiny" test, applied where legislation uses "suspect classifications." The test requires the state to show that the law satisfies a compelling state interest and that it does so in a narrowly tailored manner.[65]

The remand decision stirred up opponents of same-sex marriage, who correctly suspected that the final state court decision would favor same-sex marriage. Fearing that the Constitution's Full Faith and Credit Clause[66] could be interpreted to require all states to recognize same-sex marriages in Hawaii, or any other state that allows same-sex marriage, opponents persuaded Congress to pass the Defense of Marriage Act of 1996. Section 2 stipulated: "No state . . . shall be required to give effect to any public act, record, or judicial proceeding of any other State . . . respecting a relationship between persons of the same sex that is treated as a marriage under the laws of such other state."[67]

Before *Obergefell*, constitutional scholars differed over whether section 2 of DOMA was compatible with the Full Faith and Credit clause, although most agreed that a state was not obliged to recognize marriages contrary to its "strong public policy." Those scholars who disagreed with the "strong public policy" exception suggested a "choice of laws" approach that would have allowed a state to recognize only marriages that are consistent with a couple's common domicile. That would allow any state that did not allow same-sex marriage to not recognize such a marriage between two of its citizens who traveled to Massachusetts, let's say, to get married and then returned to their state of domicile.[68] Another scholar argued that the Full Faith and Credit Clause originally referred to "only a minor evidentiary command to the states" regarding statutes, records, or judgments.[69]

Whether or not Congress needed to pass section 2 of DOMA to guarantee that each state may define its own marriage laws and is not bound to recognize marriages from another state that violate its public policy, its passage reflected the importance of federalism in American government. Interestingly, when Congress passed section 3 of DOMA, which defined marriage as the union of a man and a woman for federal (benefits) purposes, it acted contrary to the very federalism principle it affirmed in section 2.[70]

Shortly after DOMA passed, a Hawaii trial court held the state's marriage law in violation of the state's Equal Protection Clause, staying the decision until the state supreme court could review the case. Aware of a movement to amend the state constitution on this matter, that court waited until the voters of Hawaii had passed a constitutional amendment authorizing the legislature to limit marriage to opposite-sex couples. The Hawaii Supreme Court then dismissed

the plaintiffs' action as moot, since the people of the state had constitutionalized the traditional definition of marriage.[71]

Subsequently, somewhat similar results occurred in Maine and
California; in the former case, the constitutional amendment revised
the action of the state legislature;[72] in the latter case, a constitutional
referendum revised the action of the state's supreme court.[73] Such
popular constitutional action could take place at the federal level,
but amending the federal Constitution requires a two-thirds vote
of both houses of Congress and the vote of three-quarters of state
legislatures.[74]

The Same-Sex Marriage Controversy, Pro and Con

IN THIS CHAPTER, I EXPLORE THE SAME-SEX MARRIAGE CONtroversy from the perspective of citizens and lawmakers. Here, I am interested in what is practical and wise, not what is constitutional—I assume that a law might be unwise, that is, not the best public policy, but still constitutional.[1] Constitutionality, as "legal permissibility," sets the limits of legitimate political action, but it does not determine the best policy. Yet there is no clear distinction between considerations of political wisdom and considerations of constitutionality in American government. Judicial decisions sometimes give people the impression that courts not only say what the law is, but say what it should be. That was surely the case with Justice Kennedy's court opinion in *Obergefell*.[2]

The same-sex marriage controversy illustrates the absence of a clear boundary between the legislative and the judicial spheres of government. Same-sex couples went to court and asserted their right to marry, based on the principles of equality and liberty. They sought what amounts to the right to have their loving relationships accorded the same dignity and respect that heterosexual couples receive.[3] The Supreme Court decision central to this argument was *Loving v. Virginia*, the 1967 case that invalidated state anti-miscegenation laws. Stating the position in favor of same-sex marriage reveals how constitutionality and wisdom tend to commingle. It also reveals how virtually any law in the United States that restricts individual freedom, unless it serves to directly prevent harm to others, can be put on the defensive.

While events in the 1980s caused gay rights activists to focus on marriage,[4] much of the extensive literature on same-sex marriage arose in the aftermath of a Hawaii Supreme Court decision in 1993, which led to passage of the federal Defense of Marriage Act in 1996.[5] Some of the participants in this debate revised their earlier positions, in light of the increased acceptance of same-sex marriage. But as long as the people in the several states were divided on the question of same-sex marriage, and as long as the Supreme Court had not interpreted the Constitution to require each state to recognize same-sex marriage, the controversy remained live.

At this point, the Court has decided that the Constitution requires same-sex marriage. Why should anyone consider the arguments for and against same-sex marriage now? My answer: The argument for judicial restraint, which is the key point of the four dissenting justices in *Obergefell*, must rest on something more than the assertion that the subject should be left to the political branches of government. That contention must be supported by a demonstration that the position of the political branches in those states that did not choose to enact same-sex marriage has a rational basis. If this is true, *Obergefell* should not be viewed as a model for future Supreme Court decisions affecting controversial rights claims. In this chapter, I want to provide enough of the debate over same-sex marriage to demonstrate that more than hostility to homosexuals supported and accounted for the widespread opposition to same-sex marriage.

The controversy over same-sex marriage can be divided into two distinct inquiries. The first concerns the very nature of marriage: is it rightly understood as the union of a man and a woman? The second concerns a practical consideration of the possible benefits and drawbacks to an extension of marriage to include same-sex couples.

I begin my examination of the subject by looking at the positions that focus on the first question. These positions are based either on scriptural authority or moral philosophy. Scriptural authority is important because it accounts for a good deal of opposition to homosexuality, let alone to same-sex marriage.[6] At the same time, since the American polity does not incorporate Biblical strictures, such a source cannot resolve this controversy for the courts in the United States. The moral philosophic positions prominent in this controversy have been the natural law positions of John Finnis, Robert George, and others, and the political liberalism position of John Rawls and his followers.

Finnis and the "new natural lawyers," as they are called,[7] present an argument in support of the Biblical position, but it is based on human reason alone. Rawls, in the name of finding the widest possible common ground, eschews reliance on any comprehensive moral teaching, religious or philosophic, to settle political or constitutional issues.

Moral Philosophy: The New Natural Lawyers

Finnis, George, et al. present an argument which originates in the natural law teaching of Thomas Aquinas. Their revision eliminates any reference to divine providence but also any suggestion of natural ends, or a natural teleology. For example, Aquinas derived natural law from eternal law, where eternal law referred to God's knowledge and his plan for the world and its creatures. Natural law was that part of eternal law that man, as created in God's image, could participate in through his God-given reason. In the speculative realm, this involved knowledge of being; in the practical realm, it is action aimed at the good.

Aquinas then describes three precepts of natural law, reflecting three inclinations toward good things: life, procreation and raising children, and knowledge of God and living in society. The second precept provides the basis for a preference for heterosexuality.[8]

In his book *Natural Law and Natural Rights*, John Finnis claims that Aquinas's "first principles of natural law" are not "inferred from a teleological conception of nature or any other conception of nature."[9] Finnis's account merits our attention because it explains his viewpoint on the marital act and, as a result, his opposition to same-sex marriage. First, Finnis interprets Aquinas's distinction between speculative and practical wisdom to mean that knowledge of good (practical) is completely independent of knowledge of being (speculative).[10] Then he quotes Hume's criticism of moral arguments which proceed from statements of "is" and "is not" to statements of "ought" and "ought not."[11] Ten pages later, Finnis attributes the view that "the ought cannot be deduced from the is" to Aristotle and Aquinas, while wondering whether "Hume really formulated and adhered to that principle."[12] Finnis then attributes to all three philosophers the view that "the speculative discernment of 'eternal relations,' even relations of 'fitness to human nature,' leaves open the question what motive anybody has for regulating his actions accordingly." Finally, he criticizes Hume for his "failure to see that reason is an 'active principle' because one is motivated according to one's understanding of the goodness and desirability of human opportunities, including the opportunity of extending intelligence and reasonableness into one's choices and actions."[13] Since Finnis follows up this discussion with a criticism of "traditional concepts of natural law," which depend on natural teleology, it seems that he agrees in part with Hume that theory cannot inform practice but, contrary to Hume, he argues that reason is active in the sphere of practice. And he claims that neither Aristotle's nor Aquinas's accounts of the human good depend on natural teleology.[14]

Finnis must have thought that his argument for justice and the common good would be more persuasive to a modern audience if he jettisoned anything from Plato, Aristotle, or Aquinas that either drew on natural teleology or presented the best life as intellectual, not moral. However, as one sympathetic reader has pointed out, Finnis deprived himself of reliance on "any peremptory advantage that might follow from the facts of human biology viewed from a scientific or metaphysical point of view."[15] Moreover, Finnis did not even include marriage as a basic human good in *Natural Law and Natural Rights*.[16] When he does address marriage as a human good, Finnis presents an argument that is much stricter than any that we might find in Plato or Aristotle. While it resembles Aquinas,

Finnis's argument emphasizes what he calls the "marital act" (traditional heterosexual intercourse) without regard to procreation. As a result he not only opposes same-sex marriage but also disapproves of any form of sexual activity the purpose of which is pleasure. Finnis insists on the importance of the marital act regardless of whether procreation is even possible.[17] This is to avoid any reliance on natural ends. He then must insist on the importance of the marital act by itself to support his opposition to same-sex marriage. But it is difficult to understand the difference between a physical union of two bodies in a "marital position" and two bodies in any other position if one has discounted the purpose of the marital position, namely procreation.[18]

Robert P. George and Gerald Bradley hold the same view. "The intrinsic intelligible point of the sexual intercourse of spouses, however, is, in our view, marriage itself, not procreation considered as an end to which their sexual union is the means."[19] Likewise, Sherif Girgis, Ryan T. Anderson, and Robert P. George, in their recent book *What Is Marriage? Man and Woman: A Defense*, while eschewing any condemnation of homosexuality, write: "a marital act between two people must combine the right *behavior* with the right *intention*. It must be a *real bodily union* (coitus) that seals a certain kind of union of minds and hearts." Moreover, for an act of bodily union to constitute "an act of *marital* union," the couple "need not choose it for the sake of conceiving, but simply to embody, or make concrete, their marriage: their specific, marital form of love, their permanent and exclusive commitment."[20]

This emphasis on achieving a distinctive "common good" in the marital act, without regard to the generation of life, resembles Aristotle's account of the requirements of acts of moral virtue. But it seems strange, and very unlike Aristotle, to define marriage in strictly moral terms, where the procreative end is not important and the pleasure of sexual intercourse with one's mate is condemned unless it is simply the byproduct of the marital act. That seems to be the position of Finnis and the other "new natural lawyers."[21] A better way to argue for the distinctiveness of marriage as the union between a man and a woman would seem to be to emphasize procreation, as Susan Shell does.[22] And a better way to justify allowing sterile couples to marry, but not same-sex couples, would note the impracticality and inappropriateness of trying to separate out the heterosexual couples who can and will have children from those who cannot or will not.

Finnis's position may be based on more than his strained interpretation of a marital act. Toward the end of his essay, he explicitly rejects the contention that a committed homosexual relationship can partake of the same fulfilling happiness that a heterosexual relation can. His rejection, in an essay written in 1995 and revised in 1997, contends that only a small proportion of homosexuals attempt to establish marital relationships that would involve an exclusive partnership and "the proportion that find that the attempt makes sense, in view of the other aspects of their 'gay identity,' is even tinier."[23] Advocates of gay marriage reject this assertion, and the number of same-sex marriages in the states that then allowed it contradicts that view. Finnis tries to defend it by referring to the importance of children for the institution of marriage.[24] But he cannot stick with that position, since his argument does not rely on procreation as the purpose of marriage. He then asserts that sterile couples can "still opt for this [marital] form of life as one that makes good sense."

> Given the bodily, emotional, intellectual, and volitional complementarities with which that combination of factors we call human evolution has equipped us as men and women, such a commitment can be reasonable as a participation in the good of marriage in which these infertile spouses, if well-intentioned, would wish to have participated more fully than they can. By their model of fidelity within a relationship involving acts of the reproductive kind, these infertile marriages are, moreover, strongly supportive of marriage as a valuable social institution.[25]

Thus, as important as children are for keeping married couples together and faithful, heterosexual couples that cannot have children can still have good marriages while homosexual couples cannot. Why would Finnis think that—especially since many homosexual couples wish to marry and some of them also want to have children, via adoption or the use of in vitro fertilization and/or surrogacy? Finnis's final argument is that "those who propound the homosexual ideology have no principled moral case to offer against (prudent and moderate) promiscuity, indeed the getting of orgasmic sexual pleasure in whatever friendly touch, or welcoming orifice (human or otherwise) one may opportunely find it."[26] But Finnis's view of promiscuous sexual pleasure would seem to extend to married couples' sexual intercourse, unless it is subordinated to the "marital act." Moreover, Finnis's reference to "homosexual ideology" seems to deny the generally accepted view today that sexual orientation has a genetic component and, in most cases, is firmly established at an early age.[27]

Moral Philosophy: Rawls's "Public Reason" and the Same-Sex Marriage Debate

The other argument from moral philosophy that has been prominent in the academic debate over same-sex marriage comes from John Rawls. Rawls's first book, *A Theory of Justice*,[28] laid out two principles of liberty, which derived from the social contract theories of Locke, Rousseau and Kant. In place of a state of nature, Rawls posited that individuals, starting from a hypothetical "veil of ignorance," wherein they would not know their social circumstances, physical attributes, or natural talents, thinking about themselves alone, would choose (1) equality in basic rights and duties and (2) "since everyone's well-being depends upon a scheme of cooperation without which no one could have a satisfactory life," "inequalities of wealth and authority are just only if they result in compensating benefits for everyone, and particularly for the least advantaged members of society."[29] Rawls describes this conception as "justice as fairness," because "it nullifies the accidents of natural endowment and the contingencies of social circumstance as counters in the quest for political and economic advantage."[30]

Rawls revised his position slightly in *Political Liberalism*. Justice as Fairness is now a political conception of justice, not a comprehensive moral and political account, as it was in *Theory of Justice*. It is offered to account for the overlapping consensus that is possible among adherents of different reasonable comprehensive doctrines, be they based on religion or moral philosophy. The next step is critical. In political and judicial consideration of issues for deliberation and decision, the participants must limit themselves to arguments from what Rawls calls "public reason." This means the arguments cannot depend on comprehensive doctrines, since people do not agree on them. Rawls describes his Justice as Fairness as a "free standing conception of political justice" which is detached from any comprehensive moral doctrine. To explain this change, Rawls discusses reciprocity and overlapping consensus.[31] Reciprocity requires that we give reasons that are based on principles others, holding different comprehensive views of the good, would accept. The merely political concept of justice, according to Rawls, limits itself to the overlapping consensus among the variety of reasonable comprehensive doctrines. Since public reasoning may involve conflicting comprehensive frameworks, the critical question becomes, what is the range of permissible reasonable arguments? Rawls does allow for other views of justice, or other "liberalisms," as he calls them,[32] but he is not very forthcoming about them. He allows legislators, judges, and other public officials or candidates for office to draw on reasonable comprehensive doctrines, be they theological or philosophic, but he adds, as a proviso, that the same position must be stated in a manner free from such formulations. Since his view of justice rejects any considerations from interest, and since the second principle rejects any claim that may arise from natural ability, it is not clear whether arguments on behalf of the "rational and industrious," to use Locke's terms, or utility, or natural law may be legitimately framed. That is, can these positions be expressed in a "free standing way," apart from a comprehensive doctrine? When Rawls considers a fair distribution of income, he allows for qualifications for office, without indicating whether that allows for strict competition for senior civil service jobs, but then he rules out "moral desert," since "the moral worth of character," which could comprehend ability and effort, is rejected as "including comprehensive doctrines."[33] Rawls says precious little about this, but what he does say confirms a suspicion that much is excluded from legitimate consideration. And the key effect of such an argument, if it is accepted, is to cause judges to think about and decide constitutional questions along the lines of Rawls's Justice as Fairness. When Rawls divides what he calls "the public political forum" into three parts—judges, executives and legislators, and candidates—he writes: "the idea of public reason applies more strictly to judges than to others . . . but . . . the requirements are always the same."[34] Rawls makes no distinction between political and judicial prudence. While legal realists attribute decisions to interest and Rawls advocates decisions based on principles, both parties seem to share the view that what judges do, or should do, is no different from what officials with political authority do or should do.

Rawls mentions the family in two places in his revised statement on public reason, and in each case the discussion touches on same-sex marriage.[35] In his discussion concerning the content of public reason, he describes the state's legitimate interest in the family as an institution "needed to reproduce political society over time," by "rearing and educating children."[36] From there Rawls asserts that the government would appear to have no interest in the particular form of family life, or of relations among the sexes, except in so far as that form or those relations in some way affect the orderly reproduction of society over time. Thus appeals to monogamy, or against same-sex marriages, as within the government's legitimate interest in the family, would reflect religious or comprehensive moral doctrines. Accordingly, that interest would appear improperly specified. Of course, there may be other political values in the light of which such a specification would pass muster; for example, if monogamy were necessary for the equality of women, or same-sex marriages destructive to the raising and educating of children.[37] Thus, under Rawls's political liberalism, the traditional practice of marriage is presumptively invalid; proponents of monogamy as well as marriage as the union of a man and a woman must assume the burden of proof in justifying what are regarded at the outset as presumptively violations of political liberalism. Rawls says the same thing when he discusses the family ten pages later. Writing about "the question of gay and lesbian rights and duties" in relation to families, he says: "If these rights and duties are consistent with orderly family life and the education of children, they are ceteris paribus, fully admissible."[38] Thus does Rawls dispose of the same-sex marriage controversy.

Other Arguments about Same-Sex Marriage

Most participants in the same-sex marriage debate presuppose that marriage is a positive and important institution for civil society. They differ over the proper definition of marriage, not from some set moral philosophic position but on the basis of arguments concerning the benefits and/or drawbacks, as they understand them.

Starting with the opponents, James Q. Wilson, in *The Marriage Problem: How Our Culture Has Weakened Families*, writes: "By a family I mean a lasting, socially enforced obligation between a man and a woman that authorizes sexual congress and the supervision of children. . . . A marriage is a ceremony that makes, or at least symbolizes, the legitimacy of the family."[39] At the end of his chapter "Why Do Families Exist?" Wilson notes that while the family "now rests almost entirely on affection and child care," whereas it used to be a more comprehensive "political, economic, and educational unit," it remains "a socially arranged solution for the problem of getting people to stay together and care for children that the mere desire for children, and the sex that makes children possible, does not solve."[40] David Blankenhorn, author of *The Future of Marriage*, defines the institution as Wilson does.[41]

Advocates of same-sex marriage, while agreeing with Wilson and Blankenhorn on the desirability of marriage as an institution, play down the importance of raising children and give greater weight to the social recognition of a committed loving relationship and the function of lifetime care-giving. Jonathan Rauch puts it this way in his book *Gay Marriage*: "If marriage has any meaning at all, it is that when you collapse from a stroke, there will be another person whose 'job' is to drop everything and come to your aid. . . . To be married is to know there is someone out there for whom you are always first in line."[42] Susan Shell responded to Rauch's statement by noting "This belief may well express Rauch's personal needs and longings, but it has little to do with parenthood."[43] Let's assume we agree with Shell on this point. Granting, moreover, that the two different roles can come into conflict, does that make it impossible for marriage to satisfy both responsibilities? Amy Wax, who presents a sympathetic case for traditional marriage, nonetheless suggests that as people live longer and the caregiving function becomes more significant, reasonable people might reconsider same-sex marriage.[44] Robin West argues that "no fault" divorces, the availability of birth control, and legal neutrality regarding gender roles all combine to make the traditional definition of marriage anachronistic.[45] Such an argument is not likely to persuade anyone with concerns about marriage, but the question remains, what is the likely risk of extending marriage to same-sex couples? Would not couples that use artificial modes of reproduction to have children care for them? The children were surely wanted.

Some gay rights activists do not support same-sex marriage, because they oppose the institution of marriage as incompatible with true liberation.[46] But most advocates of same-sex marriage think, with E. J. Graff, that marriage is good for gays as long as "[it] (and sex) is justified not by reproduction but by love"; then, "that venerable institution [marriage] will ever after stand for sexual choice, for cutting the link between sex and diapers."[47] Likewise, Evan Wolfson, among the first advocates of same-sex marriage, contends that the radical rejecters of marriage among the gay community are in the minority. "What many gay people do not want is an all-or-nothing model imposed on their lesbian or gay identity; they want both to be gay and married, to be gay and part of the larger society. For these lesbians and gay men, being gay is not just about being different, it is about being equal."[48]

TO PURSUE THE question concerning the consequences of same-sex marriage I want to consider part of Andrew Sullivan's argument for and David Blankenhorn's argument against.

Sullivan's book *Virtually Normal* contains a critical account of four different approaches to homosexuality, which he calls prohibitionist, liberationist, conservative, and liberal. He then presents his preferred position; he calls it "formal equality," and in light of his discussion it could be called traditional liberalism. He describes liberalism as having undergone a development from the Enlightenment position, which recognizes that securing rights is not the same as guaranteeing that everyone acts rightly towards others, to an attempt, first with respect to race, and then with respect to gender and sexual orientation, to eradicate prejudice. While he expresses sympathy for the intention, Sullivan criticizes this governmental intrusion into the private sphere, by means of laws aimed at preventing discrimination by individuals, that is, nongovernmental actors, in the areas of housing or employment. Sullivan argues for what he calls formal equality with respect to how homosexuals are treated; his examples are military service and marriage. To make his case for same-sex marriage, Sullivan, like Rauch, emphasizes the importance of the "public recognition of a private commitment," which as a "public contract [establishing] an emotional, financial, and psychological bond between two people," is thus the same for homosexuals as for heterosexuals. He dismisses the importance of procreation on the grounds that no marriage contract depends on a couple's bearing children.[49] Sullivan essentially makes a liberal argument, one that Rawls's political liberalism accepts but the traditionalists oppose.

In his epilogue, Sullivan offers personal reflections that are moving and candid.

The timeless, necessary, procreative unity of a man and a woman is inherently denied homosexuals; and the way in which fatherhood transforms heterosexual men, and motherhood transforms heterosexual women, and parenthood transforms their relationship, is far less common among homosexuals than among heterosexuals.[50]

Sullivan goes on to offer some generalizations about homosexual culture.

The experience of growing up profoundly different in emotional and psychological makeup inevitably alters a person's self-perception, tends to make him or her more wary and distant, more attuned to appearance and its foibles, more self-conscious and perhaps more reflective. The presence of homosexuals in the arts, in literature, in architecture, in design, in fashion could be understood, as some have, as a simple response to oppression.[51]

After indicating that homosexual culture can learn "[t]he values of commitment, of monogamy, of marriage, of stability" from heterosexual culture, Sullivan describes features of homosexual relations "that could nourish the broader society as well."

The mutual nourishing and sexual expressiveness of many lesbian relationships, the solidity and space of many adult gay male relationships, the openness of the contract makes it more likely to survive than many heterosexual bonds. Some of this is unavailable to the male-female union: there is more likely to be greater understanding of the need for extramarital outlets between two men than between a man and a woman; and again, the lack of children gives gay couples greater freedom.[52]

Sullivan suggests that infidelity will be a greater threat to heterosexual than homosexual couples, male and female, and apparently only partly because heterosexual couples are likely to have children. He then elaborates and explains his book's title:

I believe strongly that marriage should be made available to everyone, in a politics of strict public neutrality. But within this model, there is plenty of scope for cultural difference. There is something baleful about the attempt of some gay conservatives to educate homosexuals and lesbians into an uncritical acceptance of a stifling model of heterosexual normality. The truth is, homosexuals are not entirely normal; and to flatten their varied and complicated lives into a single moralistic model is to miss what is essential and exhilarating about their otherness.[53]

Two thoughtful conservative critics jumped on the last two passages for the same reason. Elizabeth Kristol, after quoting them and acknowledging the benefits of marriage for homosexuals, suggested that the price would be too high: young people who are uncertain of their sexual orientation, the "waverers," "would be confronted with two equally legitimate images of adult life."[54] Even assuming, Kristol says, that one's sexual orientation is "firmly established by the age of five or six (a debatable point), this would hardly mean that sexual orientation is immune from social influence." Kristol also fears that "as society broadens the definition of 'marriage,'—and some would argue that the definition has already been stretched to the breaking point, the less seriously it will be taken by everyone."[55]

James Q. Wilson's review of *Virtually Normal* took issue with Sullivan's claim that marriage would have a domesticating effect on homosexuals. His major objection, however, focused on child-rearing. "The role of raising children is entrusted in principle to married heterosexual couples because after much experimentation . . . we have found nothing else that works as well."[56] Wilson writes that little is known about how children raised by gay couples will fare.[57] Wilson is particularly critical of the use of artificial means to produce children. Wilson concludes by indicating a clear preference for a legislative, not a judicial, solution to the problem, and he seems to favor a version of civil unions.[58]

While conservatives such as Kristol and Wilson worry about the effect of homosexual lifestyle on heterosexual marriage, David Blankenhorn, in his book *The Future of Marriage*, expresses a concern about what he calls the deinstitutionalization of marriage. This means treating marriage as a private contract between two adults, subject to conditions like any other contract. Blankenhorn, whose definition of marriage focuses on procreation and child-rearing,[59] argues that same-sex marriage will transform the institution by breaking down the three forms in the name of freedom of choice:

> The first is the form of opposites: marriage is a man and a woman. The second is the form of two: marriage is for two people. The third is the form of sex: marriage is connected to sexuality and procreation. . . . Knocking out any one of them weakens the overall institution—that's the whole point—and makes it easier to knock out the other two.[60]

As for the view that "marriage is an expression of love and commitment between two people," Blankenhorn notes that such a position, without more, has led to "marriage's declining institutional authority."[61] This indicates that Blankenhorn's concern is with families and the well-being of children, not with homosexuality. But his position on marriage has implications for same-sex marriage, as he supports a view of family life with biological ties between parents and their children. He identifies the "freedom of choice" position on marriage with society's "accept[ing] the legitimacy of artificial insemination for lesbian couples who want children. More fundamentally, society must rid itself of the idea—we might call it a 'gendered' idea—that there is anything optimal about a child growing up with her own two biological parents."[62] In addition, Blankenhorn worries that the "open marriage" approach of male homosexuals, which Sullivan acknowledged, might cause heterosexual males to follow that example.[63]

Blankenhorn elaborates on his concern about children in his chapter on "Goods in Conflict." These goods are the equal dignity of homosexuals and "the child's need to be emotionally, morally, practically, and legally affiliated with the woman and the man whose sexual union brought the child into the world."[64] Blankenhorn identifies Andrew Sullivan's interest in marriage as a means of "normalizing" the life of the homosexual and while he sympathizes with the goal, he subordinates it to the marital objective of each child's being raised by his or her biological parents. He recognizes a right to marry as a "compound right":

> The right to marry implies and carries with it the right to bear and raise children. The institution of marriage as understood by the Universal Declaration is intrinsically connected to parenthood and to the values, norms, and social expectations associated with bearing and raising children.[65]

How are the rights in conflict affected by a change in the definition of marriage (from a union of a man and a woman to a union of two people)? Here is Blankenhorn on three consequences.

> Because same-sex pair-bonding cannot produce children from the union of one spouse's eggs with the other spouse's sperm, parenting by same-sex couples in every instance relies decisively on at least one of three additional factors. The first is any of the growing number of assisted reproductive technologies. The second is the involvement of third-party participants such as sperm donors, egg donors, or surrogates. And the third is the granting of parental status to at least one member of the couple who is biologically unrelated to the child. Embracing these trends as normative clearly necessitates a redefinition of parenthood itself and therefore a thorough reformulation of the right to found a family.[66]

Thus, Blankenhorn claims that same-sex marriage threatens the institution of marriage in two ways: the necessary redefinition lends support to those who would reduce marriage to a mere private contract, and it necessarily repudiates the principle that the model family involves the biological parents raising their child or children.

So how strong is Blankenhorn's argument? When we consider what, apart from same-sex marriage, has weakened this model of marriage, such as no fault divorce, adoption, birth control, and technically assisted means of reproduction, and that these legal and technological developments appear to be well established, we wonder how much more damage same-sex marriage is likely to produce, in Blankenhorn's view. Even if we accept his contention that adoption and remarriage are remedies for a loss or a failure, the results are nonetheless that some children will be raised by non-biological parents. And as for same-sex couples, before *Obergefell* many states permitted them to raise children, and for the sake of the children, the non-biological partner could become a guardian to the child. Wouldn't such children be better off if their parents received the same legal benefits as married couples? That points at least to "civil union" or "domestic partnership" status, again for the sake of the well-being of the children. But what about the added benefit of the legitimacy of full marriage? Would Blankenhorn not have to say that extending marriage to same-sex couples to legitimize their children runs the risk of encouraging same-sex couples to use artificial means of having children, children who, in many cases, will never know their biological parents? But the effect of same-sex marriage on the number of children raised by parents who cannot satisfy the biological lineage requirement is likely to be small. That leaves unanswered the question of whether extending marriage to same-sex couples will put additional pressure on what remains of the marriage forms: the union of two people who love one another and who wish to live together and take care of one another. So far—more than two years after *Obergefell*—a movement for plural marriages has not developed.

Finally, nature seems to be on the side of marriage as Blankenhorn describes it, even if American law has loosened the obligations. I refer to two facts, as I think they can be called. First, the number of homosexuals is relatively small and constant over time, regardless of the laws.[67] Second, as common sense tells us, and as both Sullivan and Rauch have attested, the natural desire in most human beings to marry and have natural children wherever possible is not likely to be undermined by extending marriage to individuals who are not able to procreate.

Given Blankenhorn's genuine interest in the well-being of children along with his straightforward acknowledgement of the dignity of homosexuals, his public statement that he had changed his mind about opposing same-sex marriage should not have been surprising. In an op-ed piece in the *New York Times* in June 2012, he concluded that his opposition to same-sex marriage had not helped "to lead heterosexual America to a broader and more positive recommitment to marriage as an institution." Noting that "much of the opposition to gay marriage seems to stem, at least in part, from an underlying anti-gay animus," Blankenhorn decided "to help build new coalitions bringing together gays who want to strengthen marriage with straight people who want to do the same."[68]

I think Blankenhorn's decision to stop opposing gay marriage was right, because the benefits are clear and immediate for some people while the harms to others are neither clear nor immediate. However, that does not mean that the Court was right to take the decision out of the hands of the people and their representatives in the several states. This is especially so since the long term effect on children raised by same-sex couples is unknown. First, the case for same-sex marriage is stronger than the case against, largely because that result obtains some clear benefits for people without any clear harm to others. Second, because the grounds for opposition are reasonable and decent, and because we cannot know what the change in marriage will mean for children raised by same-sex couples, the decision should have been left to the legislatures in the several states, or to the people directly in those states which have popular referenda.

This conclusion presupposes something that I argue in detail in the following chapters; that with some limited exceptions to be noted, and race is the most significant one, if the courts are going to allow the legislatures appropriate leeway to deliberate and decide on what is wise public policy, they must not place such a high burden on the legislature as to require a demonstration that the means chosen to effect a given objective were the very best.

CHAPTER FOUR

The Supreme Court Decisions That Laid the Foundation for Same-Sex Marriage

I TURN NOW TO THE CONSTITUTIONAL ISSUES IN THE SAME-SEX marriage controversy. As I wrote in chapter two, because the federal Constitution's Supremacy Clause (VI, 2) is a "single-edged sword,"[1] advocates of same-sex marriage, wary of taking their case to the U.S. Supreme Court, initially pursued the alternative strategy of litigating in state courts and exclusively on state constitutional grounds.

The advocates' assumption that the federal courts would not look favorably on their constitutional argument was based on the U.S. Supreme Court's summary dismissal of a challenge to Minnesota's traditional marriage law in the 1972 case of *Baker v. Nelson*.[2] In a brief unanimous opinion the Minnesota Supreme Court had held that "the institution of marriage as a union of a man and a woman, uniquely involving the procreation and rearing of children within a family, is as old as the book of Genesis."[3] With this in mind, the Court rejected plaintiffs' contentions that the restriction of marriage to couples of the opposite sex constituted either a violation of the "fundamental right to marry" under the Due Process Clause of the Fourteenth Amendment, or an "irrational or invidious discrimination" contrary to the Equal Protection Clause of the same amendment.[4]

When the Minnesota court decided *Baker* in 1972, no U.S. Supreme Court cases supported the idea of a right to same-sex marriage. Nevertheless, some Supreme Court decisions prior to 1972, and several more after, reflect a more careful examination of legislative action. This development arose out of dissatisfaction with the extreme deference the Court had been giving to economic regulations dating back to 1937; it took the form of the introduction by the Court of different levels of review, or "scrutiny," that legislation would be subjected to, depending on the classification or right involved. This included race- and then gender-based classifications that were challenged under the Fourteenth Amendment's Equal Protection Clause and fundamental rights claims that were asserted under the Due Process Clauses of the Fifth and Fourteenth Amendments. Eventually, the Court developed three distinct levels of scrutiny, known as "rational basis," "heightened," and "strict." Among the cases the Court decided using these new levels of scrutiny were two important ones in support of gay rights, *Romer v. Evans* in 1996[5] and *Lawrence v. Texas* in 2003.[6] The tighter judicial scrutiny in a range of cases and these two gay rights decisions made it possible for state and then federal courts eventually to reconsider the constitutionality of limiting marriage to the union of a man and a woman. As a prologue to a consideration of those same-sex marriage cases in the next two chapters, I first discuss these important prior decisions.

The Supreme Court's first account of what is now called "rational basis" standard for assessing the constitutionality of legislation came from Chief Justice Marshall in his opinion for the Court in *McCulloch v. Maryland* (1819), the case which upheld Congress's authority to establish a national bank: "Let the end be legitimate, let it be within the scope of the constitution, and all means which are appropriate, which are plainly adapted to that end, which are not prohibited, but consist with the letter and spirit of the constitution, are constitutional."[7] Despite disagreement about its application, the Court's "reasonableness," or "rational basis," approach to adjudicating constitutional questions remained the nominal standard for 120 years.[8]

Then in 1938, one year after the Court reversed itself by permitting state and federal regulations of the economy,[9] Justice Stone, after reaffirming a highly deferential view of the Court's "reasonableness" test, prepared the way for a more searching examination of certain categories of laws.[10] First, he suggested that the presumption of constitutionality would be less strong when the Court was confronted with specific constitutional provisions such as the right to vote or freedom of speech in contrast to the Due Process Clause. He then suggested the possible need to provide added protection for "particular religious or racial minorities" or all "discrete and insular minorities." This has come to be known as "strict scrutiny," and its first explicit use involved equal protection challenges to racial classifications. The Supreme Court first said that "all legal restrictions which shall curtail the civil rights of a single racial group are immediately suspect" in *Korematsu v. United States* (1944).[11] Ten years later, in *Bolling v. Sharpe*—the companion case to *Brown v. Board of Education*—the Court read the concept of equal protection into the Fifth Amendment's Due Process Clause and struck down racially segregated schools, affirming: "Classifications based solely upon race must be scrutinized with particular care, since they are contrary to our traditions and hence constitutionally suspect."[12] In repudiating its "separate but equal" ruling in *Plessy v. Ferguson*,[13] the Court did not quite affirm Justice Harlan's ringing statement that in matters of civil rights the "Constitution is color-blind."[14] And while the formulation emphasized scrutiny "with particular care," it continued to refer to reasonableness, rather than to use distinctive words to describe this scrutiny. But in the later affirmative action cases, the Court adopted the term "strict scrutiny," which meant "such classifications are constitutional only if they are narrowly tailored measures that further compelling governmental interests."[15] The key element in strict scrutiny concerns the closeness of the "fit" between what the law or government policy does and its stated purpose.

The Court's evolving treatment of cases involving sex discrimination, or classifications by sex, led to the current three-tiered approach to levels of judicial scrutiny. The development of the intermediate level (though the last to be articulated) arose out of two sex discrimination cases in 1971 and 1973.[16] In those cases, the Court purported to use rational basis review to invalidate laws that treated women differently from men, but the judicial scrutiny was more searching than the Court had employed in earlier cases that involved regulation of the economy.[17] Then, in *Craig v. Boren* (1976), the Court expressly introduced the third (middle) level of scrutiny, dubbed "heightened scrutiny," while invalidating a law that set higher minimum ages for the purchase of low alcohol beer for men than for women: "[To] withstand constitutional challenge previous cases [referring to *Reed* and *Frontiero*] establish that classifications by gender must serve important governmental objectives and must be substantially related to achievement of those objectives."[18] In the most recent sex discrimination cases, the Court has articulated this "heightened scrutiny" to require "an exceedingly persuasive justification."[19]

At least two justices have expressed doubts about the wisdom of the tiered approach. In his concurring opinion in *Craig v. Boren*, Justice Stevens wrote: "There is only one Equal Protection Clause. [I] am inclined to believe that what has become known as the two-tiered analysis of equal protection claims does not describe a completely logical method of deciding cases, but rather is a method the Court has employed to explain decisions that actually apply a single standard in a reasonably consistent fashion."[20] Justice Thurgood Marshall expressed a similar criticism in two other equal protection cases. In one case, the Court upheld public school funding by local property taxes, which resulted in disparate per-pupil expenditures among rich and poor districts; in the other, the Court upheld dollar limits on welfare payments to families with dependent children.[21] Since Justice Marshall dissented in both cases, his interest may have been in finding a way to scrutinize more rigorously a wider range of cases, whereas Justice Stevens may simply have thought that the differential approach obfuscated a straightforward judicial consideration of the merits of the case. In the cases involving homosexuality, we shall see the Court move toward Justice Stevens's position—and perhaps also toward Justice Marshall's.

The Court did restrain itself from expanding the categories of cases subject to higher than rational basis scrutiny in *City of Cleburne v. Cleburne Living Center* (1985).[22] There it unanimously struck down a local zoning ordinance that required permits (which had been denied) for a group home for the mentally retarded but not for apartment houses, multiple dwellings, boarding houses, fraternities, sororities, nursing homes, etc., but it specifically declined, by 5-to-4, to add mental retardation to the list of "quasi-suspect" classifications. In his court opinion, Justice White wrote that the normal presumption of constitutionality "when social or economic legislation is at issue" "gives way . . . when a statute classifies by race, alienage, or national origin," since "[t]hese factors are so seldom relevant to the achievement of any legitimate state interest that laws grounded in such considerations are deemed to reflect prejudice and antipathy—a view that those in the burdened class are not as worthy or deserving as others."[23] Justice White then mentioned gender and illegitimacy as two burdened classes: the former "generally provides no sensible ground for differential treatment," and the latter is "beyond the individual's control" and is not related to the ability to contribute to society.[24] But he thought that mental retardation was not a good candidate for special status because members in the class tend to have a "reduced ability to cope with and function in the everyday world."[25] In his concurrence, Justice Stevens reiterated his objection to the levels of scrutiny approach, which was by then threefold. While Stevens used the language of rational basis, he applied more heft to it than the Court had in earlier cases.

[In] every equal protection case, we have to ask certain basic questions. What class is harmed by the legislation, and has it been subjected to a "tradition of disfavor" by our laws? What is the public purpose that is being served by the law? What is the characteristic of the disadvantaged class that justifies the disparate treatment? In most cases the answer to these questions will tell us whether the statute has a "rational basis."[26]

Justice Marshall's partial concurrence and partial dissent called for adding mental retardation to the quasi-suspect category. He suggested that the Court was effectively using heightened scrutiny to invalidate the law but without saying so.[27]

Romer v. Evans (1996) indicates that the Court has tightened up rational basis analysis, if it has not altogether submerged heighted scrutiny into rational basis analysis. The case involved Colorado's Amendment 2, a state constitutional referendum that "deleted" all state and local laws protecting homosexuals and bisexuals against discrimination. The amendment had passed by popular referendum by a 53 percent to 47 percent vote. The Court majority, in an opinion by Justice Kennedy, struck down the amendment on equal protection grounds without, however, holding that sexual orientation was a suspect or quasi-suspect (meaning subject to heightened scrutiny) classification.

In his court opinion, Justice Kennedy noted that Colorado's approach to discrimination was to enumerate those classes of individuals that require special protection in specific laws. These included "age, military status, marital status, pregnancy, parenthood, custody of a minor child, political affiliation, physical or mental disability of an individual or of his or her associates and, in recent times, sexual orientation."[28] Amendment 2 deleted one, and only one, protected category; moreover the way it was done, by constitutional referendum, meant that no law could be passed reversing this action except with another constitutional amendment, and a state-wide majority had just expressed itself against such protection. Such an action invited discrimination in housing and places of privately owned public accommodation, as well as private employment. Since the effect of the amendment was far more extensive than what would have been needed to guarantee any legitimate concerns—such as personal or religious objections to homosexuality—the majority concluded that "the amendment seems inexplicable by anything but animus toward the class that it affects; it lacks a rational relationship to legitimate state interests."[29] In conclusion: "A State cannot so deem a class of persons a stranger to its laws."[30]

This approach resembles Justice Stevens's. The application to same-sex marriage is twofold: First, the Court takes a critical look at government action that harms homosexuals; second, it resists the rigidity of holding sexual orientation a suspect or quasi-suspect class.

Justice Stevens's suggested approach to Fourteenth Amendment cases is generally consistent with an argument Gerald Gunther made, based on his study of fifteen Supreme Court equal protection decisions in 1971–72. Professor Gunther found that "with only one exception, these cases found bite in the Equal Protection Clause after explicitly voicing the traditionally toothless minimal scrutiny standard." Gunther calls this "evolving doctrine," "a modestly interventionist model" and a "half-way house" between the toothless rational basis of post-1937 decisions and strict scrutiny. He advocated the development of a trend he had discovered, because "[it] requires that there be an affirmative relation between means and ends—or, in more traditional equal protection terms, that there be a genuine difference in terms of the state's objectives between the group within the classification and those without."[31]

I TURN NOW to the other source of cases leading to a reconsideration of same-sex marriage: the Supreme Court's use of the Due Process Clause to develop fundamental rights associated with privacy and autonomy—starting with contraception, then moving to abortion, and later intimate association and the right to marry.[32]

The Court first found a general "right of privacy" in the Constitution in *Griswold*, a Connecticut birth control case in 1965.[33] By a 7-to-2 vote the Court invalidated a law that criminally punished the use or counseling of birth control devices. The justices in the majority disagreed over whether a right to privacy could be found in the specific provisions of the first ten amendments, the Ninth Amendment, or the general principle of liberty embedded in the Fourteenth Amendment's Due Process Clause. Justice Harlan favored the last position, and the Court has followed his approach.[34] He had presented that position most fully in his dissent in *Poe v. Ullman* (1961), a case that addressed the same Connecticut law, where the Court had concluded that the issue was not yet "ripe" for decision.[35]

After defining "due process" as representing a balance between "respect for the liberty of the individual" and "the demands of organized society," Justice Harlan described that balance in terms of tradition: "That tradition is a living thing. A decision of this Court that radically departs from it could not long survive, while a decision that builds on what has survived is likely to be sound. No formula could serve as a substitute, in this area, for judgment and restraint."[36] Harlan went on to address the specific question of birth control in a manner that bears on same-sex marriage.

> The laws regarding marriage which provide both when the sexual powers maybe used and the legal and societal context in which children are born and brought up, as well as laws forbidding adultery, fornication and homosexual practices which express the negative of the proposition, confining sexuality to lawful marriage, form a pattern so deeply pressed into the substance of our social life that any Constitutional doctrine in this area must build upon that basis. . . . If we had a case before us which required us to decide simply, and in abstraction, whether the moral judgment implicit in the application of the present statute to married couples was a sound one, the very controversial nature of these questions would, I think, require us to hesitate long before concluding that the Constitution precluded Connecticut from choosing as it has among these various views. But . . . we are not presented simply with this moral judgment to be passed on as an abstract proposition. The secular state is not an examiner of consciences: it must operate in the realm of behavior, of overt actions, and where it does so operate, not only the underlying moral purpose of its operations, but also the choice of means becomes relevant to any Constitutional judgment on what is done.
>
> [Here] the State is asserting the right to enforce its moral judgment by intruding upon the most intimate details of the marital relation with the full power of the criminal law.[37]

While Justice Harlan's approach to such liberty issues was more supportive of government than Justice Stevens's approach to equal protection cases, each justice advocated balancing the interests of the government against the asserted the rights of individuals. Justices Harlan and Stevens might have come down on different sides of the question whether traditional marriage laws violate the Constitution, but each would have considered the issue directly, without having recourse to heightened scrutiny.

Justice Harlan was no longer on the Court when it decided *Eisenstadt v. Baird* in 1972[38] and extended *Griswold* to include the right of an individual, married or single, to *obtain* contraception. A year later it decided *Roe v. Wade*[39] and announced that the "right of privacy . . . is broad enough to encompass a woman's decision whether to or not to terminate her pregnancy."[40] The Court went on to lay down the trimester scheme, which allowed the state to act to protect "potential life" at the point of "viability" of the fetus, roughly at the start of the third trimester. The Supreme Court upheld the essence of *Roe*, while jettisoning the trimester scheme, nineteen years later in *Planned Parenthood of Southeastern Pennsylvania v. Casey* (1992). The joint opinion of Justices O'Connor, Kennedy, and Souter contained the following statement, written by Justice Kennedy, about the liberty at issue in the case:

> Our obligation is to define the liberty of all, not to mandate our own moral code. [Our] law affords constitutional protection to personal decisions relating to marriage, procreation, contraception, family relationships, child rearing and education. [These] matters, involving the most intimate and personal choices a person may make in a lifetime, choices central to personal dignity and autonomy, are central to the liberty protected by the Fourteenth Amendment. At the heart of liberty is the right to define one's own concept of existence, of meaning, of the universe, and of the mystery of human life. Beliefs about these matters could not define the attributes of personhood were they formed under compulsion of the State.[41]

Justice Kennedy restated part of his *Casey* opinion in *Lawrence v. Texas* (2003), the case in which the Court struck down, on due process grounds, a Texas law that criminally punished, as "deviate sexual intercourse," acts of sodomy, that is, oral or anal intercourse.[42] The Court decided the case without determining whether there was a fundamental right to engage in sodomy. Rather, in reconsidering and reversing its 1986 decision in *Bowers v. Hardwick*,[43] the Court repudiated such an approach: the question was not, as the *Bowers* Court had put it, whether there was a recognized right to engage in sodomy, but whether the liberty that is protected by the Due Process Clause covers cases "[w]hen sexuality finds overt expression in intimate conduct with another person. . . ."[44]

In repudiating Bowers, the Court noted that, while the historical practice was not so much against homosexuality as against sodomy, the laws against sodomy "do not seem to have been enforced against consenting adults acting in private."[45] Still, the Court acknowledged that "there have been powerful voices to condemn homosexual conduct as immoral." The majority opinion went on to say that "the issue is whether the majority may use the power of the State to enforce these views on the whole society through operation of the criminal law."[46]

In answer to that rhetorical question, Justice Kennedy referred to the 1955 American Law Institute's Model Penal Code, which "did not recommend or provide for 'criminal penalties for consensual sexual relations conducted in private.'" He went on to cite the European Court of Human Rights for the same position, and he noted that the number of states prohibiting sodomy had been reduced from 25 to thirteen, "of which four enforce their laws only against homosexual conduct."[47]

Justice Kennedy tried to separate the Court's decision in this case from the same-sex marriage controversy. First, he wrote that the statutes in both *Bowers* and *Lawrence* "seek to control a personal relationship that, whether or not entitled to formal recognition in the law, is within the liberty of persons to choose without being punished as criminals." And he concluded, "The present case does not involve whether the government must give formal recognition to any relationship that homosexual persons seek to enter."[48]

That did not satisfy Justice Scalia (dissenting), who decried the decision as "the product of a law-profession culture, that has largely signed on to the so-called homosexual agenda" and claimed that the decision "decrees the end of all morals legislation," including traditional marriage laws. Responding to Justice O'Connor's statement that the state interest in "preserving the traditional institution of marriage," in contrast to the "disapproval of same-sex relations" that its interest in criminalizing homosexual sodomy reflects, is legitimate, Justice Scalia wrote: "But 'preserving the traditional institution of marriage' is just a kinder way of describing the State's moral disapproval of same-sex couples."[49] But non-recognition need not imply moral disapproval.

Laurence Tribe, who served as counsel for *Bowers*, wrote a law review article shortly after *Lawrence* celebrating that decision's repudiation of *Bowers* and agreeing with Justice Scalia (on this point only) that the decision necessarily undermined the traditional institution of marriage. "[T]he evil targeted by the Court in *Lawrence* wasn't criminal prosecution and punishment of same-sex sodomy, but the disrespect for those the Court identified as 'homosexuals' that labeling such conduct as criminal helped to excuse."[50] The lack of respect argument resembles the human dignity contention that became prominent in the litigation over same-sex marriage, as I discuss below.

The Supreme Court's decisions in *Cleburne*, *Romer*, and *Lawrence* reflect the development of what Gunther described as "rational basis with bite" scrutiny. They may also reflect a disinclination to expand the legal categories meriting heightened scrutiny.

The final set of Supreme Court decisions that bear on same-sex marriage includes *Loving v. Virginia* (1967), *Zablocki v. Redhail* (1978), and *Turner v. Safley* (1987). These cases are important for the same-sex marriage controversy because the Court recognizes the importance of marriage and even affirms a "fundamental right to marry," which arguably merits extension to same-sex couples. In addition, the Court's striking down of laws that prevented interracial marriage in *Loving* was offered as strong precedent for a decision outlawing the legal prohibitions on same-sex marriage.

Loving, decided in 1967, involved the most difficult form of race-based legislation. The Virginia statutes at issue in the case prohibited marriage between "a white person and a colored person" and provided criminal punishment if such marriages occurred in the state, or if such a couple left the state to marry and then returned. The Lovings did that and were subsequently indicted, found guilty, and sentenced to a year in prison; the sentence was suspended on condition that they leave the state and not return. From their residence in the District of Columbia, the Lovings sued to have their sentence overturned. When the Virginia Court of Appeals upheld the constitutionality of the anti-miscegenation statutes, the Lovings appealed to the U.S. Supreme Court. The Court unanimously struck down the statutes, primarily on Equal Protection Clause grounds, with references to *Brown v. Board of Education* and *Korematsu*, the first case in which the Court held that race classifications were subject to the "most exact scrutiny."[51] To the state's contention that equal protection was satisfied by treating white and colored alike, the Court replied that the language of the state court decision upon which that argument was based contained language reflective of "an endorsement of the doctrine of White Supremacy."[52] And later in part one of his court opinion, Chief Justice Warren wrote: "There can be no doubt that restricting the freedom to marry solely because of racial classifications violates the central meaning of the Equal Protection Clause."[53]

In the final and short second part of his unanimous opinion, Chief Justice Warren noted that the statutes also violated the Due Process Clause because "the freedom to marry has long been recognized as one of the vital personal rights essential to the orderly pursuit of happiness by free men."[54] Warren went on to quote from *Skinner v. Oklahoma* (1942) that marriage is "one of the 'basic civil rights of man,' fundamental to our very existence and survival." He did conclude, however, by bringing the matter back to race: "Under our Constitution, the freedom to marry, or not marry, a person of another race resides with the individual and cannot be infringed by the State."[55]

In *Skinner*, the Court had struck down a sterilization law, saying, "Marriage and procreation are fundamental to the very existence and survival of the race."[56] I mention that to emphasize that the Court's statement about the importance of marriage presupposed that the institution was defined by the union of a man and a woman for the sake of procreation and raising of children.[57]

Advocates of same-sex marriage regard their cause as the most recent version of the struggle for civil rights. An analogy between race and sexual orientation, however, made in this context, presupposes that a liberal democracy has no more cause for taking into account the natural difference between male and female than it does the natural difference in race or color. Since procreation depends on a "division of labor" between male and female and has nothing to do with racial difference or similarity, it should not be assumed that a right to racially mixed marriage foretells a right to same-sex marriage.

In *Zablocki v. Redhail* (1978),[58] Justice Marshall delivered the opinion of the Court, striking down a Wisconsin law that prohibited any person who was delinquent in child custody payments from marrying without first getting a court's approval. Justice Marshall cited *Loving* for the fundamental right to marry and concluded that the state law failed to satisfy the heightened burden of proof because there were less intrusive means of furthering the state's important interests in protecting the welfare of "out-of custody" children.[59] These means included wage assignments, civil contempt, and criminal penalties. Justice Marshall also pointed out that all the law did in this case was to prevent the individual, who had no funds, from marrying.

In concurrence, Justices Stewart and Powell both objected to the breadth of the Court's "fundamental right to marry" declaration. Their approach would have acknowledged a liberty interest under the Due Process Clause and then focused on the effect of such a law on poor individuals who desired to marry.[60]

Notwithstanding the breadth of the holding regarding the fundamental right to marry, Justice Marshall's court opinion resembles *Loving* and *Skinner* in associating marriage with procreation.[61]

Finally, in 1987 in *Turner v. Safley*,[62] the Court dealt with two issues concerning rights of prisoners, one of which pertained to marriage. A Missouri law allowed inmates to marry only with the permission of the superintendent, who was authorized to grant permission for compelling reasons, such as pregnancy or birth of an illegitimate child. Justice O'Connor wrote the court opinion striking down the marriage restriction (the Court was unanimous on this issue). Noting the limitations imposed on the privacy and behavior of inmates, Justice O'Connor observed that there were many other consequences of marriage, including financial benefits as well as emotional support. But she added that "most inmates eventually will be released by parole or commutation, and therefore most inmate marriages are formed in the expectation that they ultimately will be fully consummated."[63]

I conclude this chapter with the observation that the Court's equal protection and due process decisions in areas related to same-sex marriage focus our attention on the purpose of marriage on the one hand and the relative merits of a "levels of scrutiny" versus a "balancing" approach to the adjudication of claims under either the Equal Protection or the Due Process Clause on the other hand. By "balancing," I refer to what Gunther first diagnosed, in his 1972 law review article, as a judicial scrutiny that would look carefully into the relationship between the government's stated objectives and the means chosen to attain those objectives.

Since I have discussed the Court's development of "intermediate," or "heightened" scrutiny to treat sex discrimination cases, I want to note that some lawyers and judges have argued that traditional marriage laws can be attacked as examples of sex discrimination, in which case the proper level of scrutiny would be heightened. While such an approach was briefly discussed in the *Obergefell* oral argument, the Supreme Court did not decide the case on that basis, just as no court decision, state (except for Hawaii) or federal, was based on that argument. I think the reason is that the judicial cases involving sex discrimination always involved some differential treatment between men and women. The differential treatment at issue with marriage laws concerns the sexual orientation of two people. Since marriage was traditionally defined as the union of a man and a woman for the purpose of procreation and raising children, the classification, or discrimination, is between opposite-sex and same-sex couples. Practically speaking, it is between people attracted to members of the opposite sex and those attracted to members of their own sex. Hence, the more accurate description is classification, or discrimination, by sexual orientation. Whether or not that should be allowed under the Constitution leads to the inquiry into the nature and purpose of marriage.

The Supreme Court's expansion of the categories of cases requiring more than the standard rational basis scrutiny of legislation affects judicial review in general and in its application to same-sex marriage in particular. The heightening of the level of scrutiny makes it difficult to distinguish between a legislative judgment concerning the wisdom of a measure and judicial judgment concerning its constitutionality. Prior to *Obergefell*, while the Supreme Court had not concluded that sexual orientation was subject to heightened scrutiny, some state courts, drawing either on what the Supreme Court had said about the criteria for such a classification, or on the Court's decisions regarding the fundamental right to marry, had applied at least heightened scrutiny to traditional marriage laws, and then invalidated them. After the Supreme Court's *Obergefell* decision, state courts are likely to find sexual orientation a quasi-suspect classification.

CHAPTER FIVE

Same-Sex Marriage and the Highest State Courts 1993–2009

THE U.S. SUPREME COURT'S DECISION IN OBERGEFELL SETTLED the issue of same-sex marriage throughout the United States. Nevertheless, a study of earlier decisions of state high courts—before the issue became federal—reveals the full range of *possible* judicial resolutions to the question. Because the different decisions and the opinions that accompanied them informed federal judges when the issues came before their courts, it will be worthwhile to look at some of those state cases.

From 1993 to 2009, the highest courts in ten states decided cases involving same-sex marriage: Hawaii (1993),[1] Vermont (1999),[2] Massachusetts (2003),[3] New York (2006),[4] Washington (2006),[5] New Jersey (2006),[6] Maryland (2007),[7] California (2008),[8] Connecticut (2008),[9] Iowa (2009).[10] These state court decisions can be classified on the basis of three broadly different outcomes. The courts in Vermont and New Jersey held that their state constitutions required that equal benefits be available to same-sex couples, but not marriage.[11] The courts in Hawaii, Massachusetts, California, Connecticut, and Iowa held that their constitutions required that same-sex couples be allowed to marry.[12] The courts in New York, Washington, and Maryland held that their states' traditional marriage laws were not unconstitutional, and that any change would have to come from the legislature.[13] Furthermore, with the exception of Iowa, in which the court unanimously held that same-sex marriage must be allowed, each state court divided closely.[14]

To provide a full range of the state judges' opinions in these cases, while minimizing repetition of the constitutional arguments they addressed, I focus on one case from each category: those from Vermont, Massachusetts, and New York. I also look at Hawaii and California. Hawaii's was the first case; it led directly to the passage of the federal Defense of Marriage Act and provoked a constitutional amendment rescinding the state court's decision.[15] California's case also provoked a constitutional amendment, Proposition 8, and led to the issue becoming a federal question.[16]

A. Hawaii

In *Baehr v. Lewin* (1993), the Supreme Court of Hawaii considered two issues: whether the state constitution's "right of the people to privacy" included the fundamental right to marry, and therefore made the statute's references to "husband" and "wife" invalid; and whether the state constitution's Equal Protection Clause made sex a suspect classification, which would require application of strict scrutiny to a state law that limited marriage to the union of a man and woman.[17] In his opinion for the court, Justice Levinson interpreted the U.S. Supreme Court precedent on the fundamental right to marry to apply only to couples capable, in principle, of procreating, that is, heterosexual couples.[18] But then he labeled Hawaii's marriage law to be a sex-based classification, and he interpreted the state's constitution to treat such classifications as "suspect,"[19] and hence subject to strict scrutiny.[20] The case was then remanded to the trial court.[21]

After the Hawaii Supreme Court ruling, opponents of same-sex marriage foresaw that, on remand, the trial court would find Hawaii's marriage in violation of the Hawaii constitution's Equal Protection Clause. (In fact this is what eventually happened.) They feared that other state courts might then conclude that the Full Faith and Credit Clause of the U.S. Constitution required that even states which prohibited same-sex marriage would have to recognize such marriages—between persons who were domiciled in those states, after having been (legally) married in Hawaii.[22]

Those opponents called for Congressional hearings with a view toward preventing that outcome. Hearings were held in Washington, and they resulted in the passage of the Defense of Marriage Act of 1996. Section 2 addressed the Full Faith and Credit issue expressly by exempting the states from the requirement of giving effect to same-sex marriages contracted in any other state.[23]

Shortly thereafter, the Hawaii legislature initiated a state constitutional amendment—ratified and adopted in 1998—which affirmed the legislature's authority to limit marriage to opposite sex couples.[24]

In the meantime, on remand the Hawaii trial court ruled in favor of same-sex marriage, as expected. When the case once again reached the Hawaii Supreme Court on appeal, that court recognized that the state constitutional amendment settled the question of the validity of the state's marriage law (which banned same-sex marriage) and therefore dismissed the lawsuit.[25]

Thus, Hawaii used its constitutional amendment process to assert the authority of the state's legislature to prohibit same-sex marriage when the state's supreme court had indicated that it was inclined to rule that same-sex marriage must be permitted and the state trial court had followed that position. This is, I believe, the preferred way to use the constitutional referendum, since it keeps the discretion in the representative legislative body. In other states, the constitutional referendum was used to prohibit a legislative decision for same-sex marriage.

B. The Vermont Case: *Baker v. State* and Civil Unions

Toward the end of 1999, the Vermont Supreme Court handed down its decision in *Baker v. State*.[26] In an opinion written by Chief Justice Jeffrey Amestoy, the court held the state's exclusion of same-sex couples from the benefits and protections that its laws provided to opposite-sex couples violated chapter I, article 7 of the Vermont constitution.[27] The court presented the state's legislature with the following choice: allow same-sex couples either to marry or to form "civil unions."[28] The following year, after heated debates, the Vermont Legislature enacted a civil unions bill, thus opting for the non-marriage or "marriage-lite" alternative.[29]

The *Baker* opinion did not limit the state constitution's common benefits clause to its "original meaning," which explicitly outlawed hereditary privileges.[30] It described the Vermont courts "as broadly deferential to the legislative prerogative to define and advance governmental *ends*, while vigorously ensuring that the *means* chosen bear a just and reasonable relation to the governmental objective."[31]

Chief Justice Amestoy rejected the state's argument that the marriage law served the governmental purposes of procreation and child-rearing.[32] He found the law's exclusion "significantly under-inclusive," since so many opposite-sex couples who marry either do not or cannot have children.[33] He also noted that the Vermont Legislature had earlier "acted affirmatively" to remove legal barriers so that same-sex couples could legally adopt and rear children conceived through assisted reproductive techniques.[34] In addition, the state "acted to expand the domestic relations laws to safeguard the interests of same-sex parents and their children when such couples terminate their domestic relationship."[35] Not only do many same-sex couples desire to have children through in vitro fertilization or surrogacy, but the state does not manifest any interest in restricting such techniques, which both opposite-sex and same-sex couples utilize. Chief Justice Amestoy concluded: "[T]here is no reasonable basis to conclude that a same-sex couple's use of the same technologies would undermine the bonds of parenthood, or society's perception of parenthood."[36] The Chief Justice acknowledged federal and state cases that upheld under-inclusive statutes, but he did not accept such a justification in *Baker*, because "[t]he State does not contend . . . that the same-sex exclusion is necessary as a matter of pragmatism or administrative convenience."[37]

Finally, Chief Justice Amestoy considered the state's contention that children are best reared by a man and a woman. After noting that experts disagree on such a contention, he observed that the state had undermined its own argument by "removing all prior legal barriers to the adoption of children by same-sex couples."[38]

If anything was missing from the court opinion in *Baker*, it was a full answer to Justice Johnson, who, in a separate opinion, wrote that the arguments for common benefits should have led to the finding of a constitutional right to marry.[39] The Chief Justice and the court left that question for another day, since the plaintiffs' claims and arguments focused primarily upon the consequences of official exclusion from the statutory benefits, protections, and security incident to marriage under Vermont law.[40]

After the *Baker* decision was handed down, the Vermont Legislature debated and then passed a civil union bill in April 2000 by votes of 19-to-11 in the Senate and 79-to-68 in the House. Governor Howard Dean signed the bill into law on April 26.[41] Act 91 offered civil unions to couples of the same sex who were otherwise qualified, by age and absence of consanguinity, to marry.[42] Then, in 2009, the Vermont Legislature voted to approve same-sex marriage, overriding Governor Jim Douglas's veto.[43] The Vermont Supreme Court might well claim credit for the result, for it gave the legislature an opportunity to play a role, and the Legislature's decision gave the people time to experience the effect of civil unions, which probably made a vote in favor of same-sex marriage possible.[44] Otherwise, Vermont may have become embroiled in a nasty constitutional controversy, as occurred in California.

C. Massachusetts: *Goodridge v. Department of Public Health* (2003)

I turn now to the Massachusetts Supreme Judicial Court and its 2003 decision in *Goodridge v. Department of Public Health*.[45] *Goodridge* marked the first time a state high court held that a traditional marriage law violated a state's constitution by prohibiting same-sex couples to marry.[46] The Massachusetts court handed down five separate opinions in the case. Chief Justice Margaret Marshall wrote the majority opinion, which invalidated the state's marriage law on rational basis analysis.[47] Justice Greaney wrote a concurrence, applying strict scrutiny, because he interpreted the "fundamental right to marry" cases to apply to same-sex couples.[48] Justices Spina, Sosman, and Cordy each submitted a dissenting separate opinion.[49]

The first two sentences of Chief Justice Marshall's opinion establish the framework for her argument: "Marriage is a vital social institution. The exclusive commitment of two individuals to each other nurtures love and mutual support; it brings stability to our society."[50] The Chief Justice's definition of marriage moves away from procreation and the rearing of children. Using this new, and broader, definition of marriage, she writes: "The question before us is whether, consistent with the Massachusetts Constitution, the Commonwealth may deny the protections, benefits, and obligations conferred by civil marriage to two individuals of the same sex who wish to marry. We conclude that it may not."[51] After describing both sides of the controversy as reflecting "deep-seated [or] strong religious, moral, and ethical convictions," Chief Justice Marshall states, in a manner echoing Rawls's "public reason": "Our concern is with the Massachusetts Constitution as a charter of governance for every person properly within its reach."[52] This is followed by a quotation from Justice Anthony Kennedy's recent opinion in *Lawrence v. Texas*: "'Our obligation is to define the liberty of all, not to mandate our own moral code.'"[53]

"Liberty of all" in this context means choosing the less restrictive definition of marriage in order to allow for a more inclusive result. Chief Justice Marshall acknowledges that the court's decision "marks a change in the history of our marriage law,"[54] and she refers later to "the long-standing statutory understanding, derived from the common law, that 'marriage' means the lawful union of a woman and a man."[55] But, she continues, "that history cannot and does not foreclose the constitutional question."[56]

Does such a substantial rejection of tradition square with rational basis review, even the invigorated version which Gunther first recognized more than 40 years ago and which the U.S. Supreme Court has used in recent cases? Let's look at how Chief Justice Marshall argues against the state's traditional marriage law. She identifies three reasons offered by the state in support of the law—procreation, child-rearing, and preservation of scarce resources—and then adds a fourth—the concern about the "deinstitutionalization of marriage."[57] The first two reasons, which are related, are the most important.

To the first argument, Chief Justice Marshall replies that the law does not privilege procreative heterosexual intercourse.[58] Why not? The proof is that there is no law requiring proof of ability or intention of a married couple to conceive children by intercourse. This idea is key to the constitutional argument for advocates of same-sex marriage. Chief Justice Amestoy cited it in the Vermont case.[59] Chief Justice Marshall notes that fertility is not a condition of marriage or divorce.[60] But wouldn't such a requirement make for a preposterously illiberal law? Isn't it enough that it is assumed that heterosexual couples will have sexual intercourse and as a result, in most cases, they will have children? A refinement on this argument, which Chief Justice Marshall does not make, would be to ask why elderly couples, in particular, why women past the childbearing age, should be allowed to marry.[61]

The second reason concerns children, namely, that the optimal family setting for children is to be raised by their biological parents, or at least by a father and a mother.[62] Here Chief Justice Marshall points out that Massachusetts has acted to unburden children from the stigma of illegitimacy.[63] But why does that move preclude a law that sets the standard as being raised by a mother and father, preferably one's biological parents? That is the position of dissenting Justices Sosman and Cordy.[64] Chief Justice Marshall's position seems to be that prohibiting marriage by same-sex couples, some of whom already have children by adoption or artificial means, stigmatizes those children in a way similar to the stigma of illegitimacy.[65] In addition, the Massachusetts majority notes that the Department of Public Health offered no evidence showing that there would be an increase in the number of same-sex couples choosing to have and raise children if they were allowed to marry.[66]

The Chief Justice acknowledged that the court's decision marked "a significant change in the definition of marriage as it has been inherited from the common law. . . ." But, she continued, "it does not disturb the fundamental value of marriage in our society."[67] In light of the intensity of popular feelings around the issue of same-sex marriage, would that not counsel against courts getting so far out in front on the issue? For the majority, however, the issue is one of civil rights, not essentially different from that of racial discrimination. The court declares: "The marriage ban works a deep and scarring hardship on a very real segment of the community for no rational reason."[68]

Justice Sosman's dissent emphasizes the significance of the change the court is making in Massachusetts' marriage laws without an adequate knowledge of the long-term effects of the change on child-rearing.[69] Noting that scientific studies on the subject have "become clouded by the personal and political beliefs of the investigators," she thinks it will be necessary to wait for studies of how those children of same-sex couples fare as adults. The majority's assumption that the sex of a child's parents is irrelevant to that child's well-being is, according to Justice Sosman, "a passionately held but utterly untested belief."[70] Therefore, "[t]he Legislature is not required to share that belief but may, as the creator of the institution of civil marriage, wish to see the proof before making a fundamental alteration to that institution."[71]

Chief Justice Marshall, in reply, describes the "history of constitutional law" as the "'story of the extension of constitutional rights and protections to people once ignored or excluded.'"[72] The Chief Justice faulted the state for failing to "articulate a constitutionally adequate justification for limiting civil marriage to opposite-sex unions."[73] The state's purported justifications for the civil marriage restriction "are starkly at odds with the comprehensive network of vigorous, gender-neutral laws promoting stable families and the best interests of children."[74] Apparently, for the majority, gender neutrality was a constitutional requirement that extends to sexual orientation and hence to marriage.

The marriage ban works a deep and scarring hardship on a very real segment of the community for no rational reason. The absence of any reasonable relationship between, on the one hand, an absolute disqualification of same-sex couples who wish to enter into civil marriage and, on the other, protection of public health, safety, or general welfare, suggests that the marriage restriction is rooted in persistent prejudices against persons who are (or who are believed to be) homosexual. The Constitution cannot control such prejudices but neither can it tolerate them. . . . Limiting the protections, benefits, and obligations of civil marriage to opposite-sex couples violates the basic premises of individual liberty and equality under law protected by the Massachusetts Constitution.[75]

In a footnote, the Chief Justice indicated that she did not mean to attribute to the originators of the common law of marriage an intent to discriminate.[76] Therefore, according to Chief Justice Marshall, the failure of the legislature to change its marriage law to permit homosexuals to marry has no rational basis and therefore must be "rooted in persistent prejudices." This is strong stuff. The case for having children raised by their biological parents is rejected, either out of hand, or with a means-end fit requirement that amounts to strict scrutiny. After all, there is no way, consistent with a respect for privacy, to limit marriage to couples that are both willing and able to procreate. As the majority views the case, it's not even close; there is no conflict of goods and no need to consider Vermont's "common benefits" approach.

D. The New York Case: *Hernandez v. Robles* (2006)

Hernandez v. Robles, decided in July of 2006,[77] is the mirror image of *Goodridge*. By a vote of 4-to-2 the highest state court upheld New York's traditional marriage law without addressing a version of civil unions or domestic partnerships.[78] Judge R. S. Smith wrote a succinct opinion defending the law and directing same-sex advocates to seek relief from the legislature.[79] Chief Judge Kaye wrote a strong dissent.[80] These two opinions differ in their general approaches and in their specific treatments of the test for fundamental rights under the Due Process Clause and in their consideration of equal protection of the laws.

Applying a rational basis test to the plaintiffs' challenge to the state's marriage law, Judge Smith supported two constitutional grounds for the state's limitation of marriage to opposite-sex couples.

> First, the Legislature could rationally decide that, for the welfare of children, it is more important to promote stability, and to avoid instability, in opposite-sex than in same-sex relationships. Heterosexual intercourse has a natural tendency to lead to the birth of children; homosexual intercourse does not.[81]

Judge Smith's second reason also concerns the well-being of children:

> The Legislature could rationally believe that it is better, other things being equal, for children to grow up with both a mother and a father. Intuition and experience suggest that a child benefits from having before his or her eyes, every day, living models of what both a man and a woman are like.[82]

As we have seen, this is a critical argument in the debate over same-sex marriage. The difference of opinion in the judicial context is not only over whether the statement is correct—advocates of same-sex marriage deny it—but also, if the answer is not clear, which side has the burden of proof. Stated differently, how close must the means-end relationship be shown to be in order to survive rational basis scrutiny?

Judge Smith denied that the state's traditional marriage law was "founded on nothing but prejudice."[83] Acknowledging the injustices perpetrated against homosexuals, he noted the state's passage of the Sexual Orientation Non-Discrimination Act four years earlier.[84] He did not regard the limitation of marriage as a violation of that act.[85] According to Judge Smith: "The idea that same-sex marriage is even possible is a relatively new one. . . . A court should not lightly conclude that everyone who held this belief [that marriage should be limited to opposite sex couples] was irrational, ignorant, or bigoted. We do not so conclude."[86]

Turning to the Due Process Clause, Judge Smith quoted Justice Souter's opinion in *Washington v. Glucksberg* to support the notion that fundamental rights are "'deeply rooted in this Nation's history and tradition.'"[87] He then concluded that while the right to marry was fundamental, the right to marry someone of the same sex was not.[88]

Judge Smith also wrote that the plaintiffs in the case, unlike those in *Lawrence*, "seek from the courts access to a state-conferred benefit that the Legislature has rationally limited to opposite-sex couples." [89] In other words, the right to intimate association did not imply the right to marry for two persons of the same sex.

Judge Smith then took up the equal protection argument. Treating the law as classification by sexual orientation,[90] he concluded, drawing on the *Cleburne* case, that rational basis applied and that the law passed that test.[91] He did say that heightened scrutiny might be appropriate for sexual orientation discrimination in some cases, "but not where we review legislation governing marriage and family relationships."[92] If some classifications based on sexual orientation are more suspicious than others, it seems to be a good reason to apply a relatively strict rational basis, which is what the U.S. Supreme Court did in *Romer*, *Glucksberg*, and *Lawrence*.

Finally, Judge Smith replied to the plaintiffs' contention that the "means-end" fit was not close enough.[93] The "under-inclusiveness" was not in violation of a rational relationship, since the greater concern was with unplanned pregnancies.[94] Nor was the "over-inclusiveness" in violation of a rational relationship, since "limiting marriage to opposite-sex couples likely to have children would require grossly intrusive inquiries, and arbitrary and unreliable line-drawing."[95]

In her dissent, Chief Judge Kaye linked same-sex marriage with civil rights: "Solely because of their sexual orientation . . . that is, because of who they love[,] plaintiffs are denied the rights and responsibilities of civil marriage. This State has a proud tradition of affording equal rights to all New Yorkers. Sadly, the Court today retreats from that proud tradition."[96] In response to the majority's decision to direct the plaintiffs to the legislature (where they eventually succeeded), Chief Judge Kaye responded: "It is uniquely the function of the Judicial Branch to safeguard individual liberties guaranteed by the New York State constitution, and to order redress for their violation. The Court's duty to protect constitutional rights is an imperative of the separation of powers, not its enemy."[97]

This formulation harkens back to a founding principle of our country, that the peculiar function of the courts is "to say what the law is."[98] The difficulty arises as courts expand the range of rights that they will enforce, and the result is a significant narrowing of the range for legislative choice regarding the desirability of a given policy. Since, as James Madison pointed out, many legislative conflicts can be framed in terms of rights, courts need to be careful about excessive encroachment on the legislative sphere.[99]

Chief Judge Kaye acknowledged that the doctrine of "fundamental rights" refers to those "'which are, objectively, deeply rooted in this Nation's history and tradition, . . . and implicit in the concept of ordered liberty, such that neither liberty nor justice would exist if they were sacrificed.'"[100] But that did not prevent her from asserting that, "fundamental rights, once recognized, cannot be denied to particular groups on the ground that these groups have historically been denied those rights."[101] She thereby assumed that "the fundamental right to marry" should apply to same-sex couples where the court's statements assumed the traditional definition of marriage.

For Chief Judge Kaye, the historical and traditional approach to fundamental rights fails because once upon a time racial segregation was supported.[102] For her, as for the Massachusetts majority in the *Goodridge*,[103] there is no difference between the race issue that was laid to rest in *Loving* and a governmental preference for heterosexuality.[104]

When she turns to equal protection, Chief Judge Kaye writes that "the question before us is not whether the marriage statutes properly benefit those they are intended to benefit—any discriminatory classification does that—but whether there exists any legitimate basis for *excluding* those who are not covered by the law."[105] She argues that "[h]omosexuals meet the constitutional definition of a suspect class" because, "[o]bviously, sexual orientation is irrelevant to one's ability to perform or contribute."[106]

Chief Judge Kaye also thought the law failed even rational basis review. In other words, it was not enough for the state to have a legitimate interest in recognizing or supporting opposite-sex marriages. Rather, "[t]he relevant question here is whether there exists a rational basis for *excluding* same-sex couples from marriage, and, in fact, whether the State's interests in recognizing or supporting opposite-sex marriages are rationally *furthered* by the exclusion."[107] To the suggestion offered by the majority that the state's concern (about unplanned pregnancies) accounts for the current marriage laws, Chief Judge Kaye replies: "There are enough marriage licenses to go around for everyone."[108]

E. California: *In re Marriage Cases* (2008)

California's same-sex marriage cases were complicated and distinctive. They were complicated by the fact that the Supreme Court of California had recently ruled that public officials in San Francisco had unlawfully issued marriage licenses to same-sex couples.[109] The California cases were distinctive, as compared with other state court cases, because the California Legislature had, in a series of acts in recent years, established domestic partnerships for same-sex couples that gave those partners virtually the same rights that married couples had.[110] Therefore the issue was not, as it was in Vermont and New Jersey, merely whether the state constitution required extending the rights of marriage to same-sex couples who wanted to marry; the issue in California was whether the rights of marriage without the title "marriage" sufficed in light of either a fundamental right to marry or the requirements of equal protection.[111]

At the outset of his opinion, in a 4-to-3 decision, Chief Judge George indicated that the fundamental right to marry extended to same-sex couples.

> [The] core substantive rights [associated with marriage] include, most fundamentally, the opportunity of an individual to establish—with the person with whom the individual has chosen to share his or her life—an *officially recognized and protected family* possessing mutual rights and responsibilities and entitled to the same respect and dignity accorded a union traditionally designated as marriage.[112]

Chief Judge George did not provide a source for the constitutional weight he applied to the terms "respect and dignity," although it seems to come from Ronald Dworkin, who himself cites Rawls.[113] The effect of such a constitutional mandate is to disallow any political compromise in the form of "civil unions" or "domestic partnerships."

In his dissent, Judge Baxter criticized the court for not allowing the California Legislature, which had enacted a generous domestic partnership plan, further time to work things out.[114] Judge Baxter claimed that the majority used its own interpretation of the legislature's acts to nullify the people's initiative.[115]

Chief Judge George wrote that it was unfair to suggest that the plaintiffs were seeking a new right, because they were not attempting "to change, modify, or . . . 'deinstitutionalize' the existing institution of marriage."[116] And yet, he acknowledged that marriage had never meant the union of any two persons.[117] Still, the majority interpreted the state legislation prohibiting discrimination on the basis of sexual orientation as reflecting an "equal legal status" that required same-sex marriage.[118] In other words, the majority's analysis of the fundamental right to marry presented a logically straightforward result that goes against, or beyond, tradition and the considered judgment of several legislatures and the people, through a legislative initiative, and requires a new definition of marriage. To the dissenting judges, this may be a change for the better, but it should come from the legislature.

When the Chief Judge addressed the "historical matter" that marriage in California has always "been limited to a union between a man and a woman," he replied that reliance on tradition alone does not suffice to justify the restriction of a fundamental right.[119] That, of course, begs the question of whether the meaning of the "fundamental right to marry" extends to two persons of the same sex. That is undoubtedly a question, since when the Supreme Court announced the doctrine it was only thinking of marriage as the union of a man and a woman.

Granting that law must evolve with changing mores and circumstances, the question is which institution of government should take the lead in initiating these changes.

Did the majority think that the failure to change the law to include same-sex couples indicated discrimination based on sexual orientation? While he did not say so explicitly, Chief Judge George did note the change in societal attitudes toward homosexuals:[120] what was considered an illness is now understood as a condition, which, while not simply determined genetically, is not freely chosen and which characterizes a small but distinct minority of the population.[121] Hence, "we now . . . recognize that an individual's homosexual orientation is not a constitutionally legitimate basis for withholding or restricting the individual's legal rights."[122] And, he might have added, marriage is simply a contract, which healthy adults have a right to enter into—subject, I suppose, to reasonable age and consanguinity restrictions.

Chief Judge George replied to David Blankenhorn's argument concerning the importance of "promot[ing] a stable relationship for the procreation and raising of children" by noting that "the constitutional right to marry never has been viewed as the sole preserve of individuals who are physically capable of having children."[123] In other words, the class of individuals who are allowed to marry is not limited to those who are able and willing to procreate. In addition, same-sex couples are able to have children "through adoption or through means of assisted reproduction."[124]

Finally, Chief Judge George found inadequate the argument that the state has a greater concern about regulating the sexual activities of heterosexuals than of homosexuals, since unintended pregnancies put children at risk, whereas same-sex couples have to plan to have children. Chief Judge George replied that by recognizing the right of same-sex couples to marry, the court does nothing to "alter or diminish either the legal responsibilities that biological parents owe to their children or the substantial incentives that the state provides to a child's biological parents to enter into and raise their child in a stable, long-term committed relationship."[125] The question, rather, is whether a democratically responsible legislature may choose to limit marriage to the family arrangements it prefers to encourage, while at the same time lending equal financial resources to same-sex couples under the domestic partnership law.[126]

Judges Baxter and Corrigan, in largely dissenting opinions (concurring only in minor parts), emphasized the significance of the break with tradition, maintaining that the change should come from the democratic process.[127] But neither opinion developed the case for the traditional position, which would require a positive argument concerning the importance of every child having a father and a mother. The majority's response to the dissents' separation of powers argument was that "a court has an *obligation* to enforce the limitations that the California Constitution imposes upon legislative measures, and a court would shirk the responsibility it owes to each member of the public were it to consider such statutory provisions to be insulated from judicial review."[128]

CHAPTER SIX

Making a Federal Case
Out of It

A. Transition: Pushback from the People

IN RESPONSE TO THE CALIFORNIA SUPREME COURT'S DECISION, the voters of California, by a 52-to-48 percent margin, approved a constitutional amendment known as Proposition 8.[1] By affirming that "Only marriage between a man and a woman is valid or recognized in California,"[2] the action nullified the court's decision in the *Marriage Cases*. Supporters of same-sex marriage then brought suit in the California Supreme Court, challenging the proposition's constitutionality.[3] The California Supreme Court had to decide whether Proposition 8 was a constitutional "amendment," and hence valid, or a constitutional "revision," and hence invalid.[4] The judges on the court, who had voted 4-to-3 that the state's constitution required same-sex marriage, now voted 6-to-1 that Proposition 8 was valid.[5]

The California Supreme Court interpreted the scope of the new constitutional provision to repeal its own holding in the *Marriage Cases* concerning the right of same-sex couples to marry, but it did not interpret the provision to in any way detract from the "familial rights of same-sex couples" that the legislature had already granted in the form of domestic partner legislation.[6]

B. Making the Federal Case: *Perry v. Schwarzenegger* (2010)

The next venue for the Proposition 8 case was federal district court in *Perry v. Schwarzenegger*,[7] with attorneys Ted Olson and David

Boies (adversaries in *Bush v. Gore* (2000))[8] joining together to represent the advocates of same-sex marriage.[9] Many same-sex marriage advocates disagreed with the decision to take the case to federal court. They believed that even if they won at the trial level, the case would eventually reach the U.S. Supreme Court, where they feared losing.[10]

District Court Judge Vaughn Walker presided over a trial that lasted from January to June 2009, and on August 4, 2009 he delivered his decision in favor of the plaintiffs.[11]

The basic arguments against Proposition 8 were, first, that it violated gay persons' fundamental right to marry; and second, that it disadvantaged homosexuals, allegedly a suspect class, and therefore violated the Equal Protection Clause.[12] The basic argument in support was that Proposition 8 intended to protect marriage[13] and was not "an attack on the gay lifestyle."[14] In his opinion, Judge Walker made it abundantly clear that he found no merit in the argument for restricting marriage to the union of a man and a woman.[15] Moreover, while he acknowledged the views of David Blankenhorn, the major expert witness offered by the proponents, he concluded that neither Blankenhorn's credentials nor his testimony qualified him as an expert witness.[16] In his Findings of Fact section, issued before the decision itself, Judge Walker indicated that he would invalidate Proposition 8 on broad constitutional grounds.[17] A telling moment in the trial occurred when Judge Walker pressed the defendants' counsel to explain how permitting same-sex marriage would adversely affect the state's interest in preserving the institution of marriage, which finally elicited the response, "I don't know. I don't know."[18] Further on in his opinion, Judge Walker used Blankenhorn's own candid acknowledgment that there would be benefits to same-sex marriage against him.[19]

In his summary of the evidence, Judge Walker identified three questions:

Whether any evidence supports California's refusal to recognize marriage between two people because of their sex; whether any evidence shows California has an interest in differentiating between same-sex and opposite-sex unions; and whether the evidence shows Proposition 8 enacted a private moral view without advancing a legitimate government interest.[20]

Addressing the first question, Judge Walker contrasted the views of historian Nancy Cott with those of Blankenhorn.[21] He presented Cott's view of marriage as

a couple's choice to live with each other, to remain committed to one another, and to form a household based on their own feelings about one another, and their agreement to join in an economic partnership and support one another in terms of the material needs of life.[22]

Then Judge Walker turned to Blankenhorn, noting that he "testified that marriage is 'a socially-approved sexual relationship between a man and a woman' with a primary purpose to 'regulate filiation'."[23] Judge Walker noted that Blankenhorn acknowledged the benefits of extending marriage to gays but opposed it because he thought the resulting harm to children would be worse.[24] Judge Walker asserted, "[t]he trial evidence provides no basis for establishing that California has an interest in refusing to recognize marriage between two people because of their sex," by which he meant two people of the same sex.[25] In elaboration, Judge Walker analogized racial restrictions to the limitation on same-sex marriage: he argued that once gender-based restrictions on employment, in the name of a division of labor, were eliminated, there was no remaining justification for the prohibition on same-sex marriage.[26] This assumes that the difference between a mother and a father is identical to the difference between a parent who works outside the home and a parent who works in the home.

Addressing the second question, concerning the state's interest in preferring opposite-sex to same-sex unions, Judge Walker cited psychologists who concluded, "same-sex couples are in fact indistinguishable from opposite-sex couples in terms of relationship quality and stability."[27] Consequently, Proposition 8 "provides state endorsement of private discrimination" and "increases the likelihood of negative mental and physical health outcomes for gays and lesbians."[28] Moreover, studies comparing families headed by same-sex couples with families headed by opposite-sex couples "show conclusively that having parents of different genders is irrelevant to child outcomes."[29]

Noting that the last point, made by Michael Lamb, a psychology professor, conflicted directly with Blankenhorn's emphasis on "the importance of biological parents," Judge Walker stated, "none of the studies Blankenhorn relied on isolates the genetic relationship between a parent and a child as a variable to be tested."[30] Lamb testified, "children conceived using sperm or egg donors are just as likely to be well-adjusted as children raised by their biological parents."[31] Judge Walker even quoted Blankenhorn as "agree[ing] with Lamb that adoptive parents 'actually on some outcomes outstrip biological parents in terms of providing protective care for their children.'"[32]

The third question concerned evidence showing that Proposition 8 enacted a private moral view without advancing a legitimate government interest.[33] Judge Walker drew from the testimony of historian George Chauncey on the history of discrimination against gays, the testimony of political scientist Gary Segura on the effect of negative stereotypes on gays, and the testimony of supporters of Proposition 8 whose arguments were based on religious beliefs.[34] Judge Walker observed, "the voters' determinations must find at least some support in evidence" and "the moral disapprobation of a group or class of citizens" will not suffice. He concluded that "[t]he evidence demonstrated beyond serious reckoning that Proposition 8 finds support only in such disapproval."[35]

Judge Walker required relatively little space to state his conclusions of law. On the due process claim, he found that the fundamental right to marry applied to same-sex couples.[36] He replied to the argument from "the history, tradition and practice of marriage" by implicitly likening the issue of same-sex marriage to that of interracial marriage.[37] He then took the elimination of legally enforced gender roles to amount to a refutation of any argument based on a natural difference between men and women.[38] He added, "[n]ever has the state inquired into procreative capacity or intent before issuing a marriage license."[39] Hence the natural difference between the sexes becomes an archaic requirement once women are legally permitted to pursue any career.[40]

Judge Walker's conclusions on these questions were based on his acceptance of the expert testimony of Lamb.[41] Lamb "offer[ed] two broad opinions[:] . . . [F]irst . . . children raised by gay and lesbian parents are just as likely to be well adjusted as children raised by heterosexual parents. And [second] . . . for a significant number of these children, their adjustment would be promoted were their parents able to get married."[42]

Drawing on more than 30 years' research, Lamb described a consensus on three factors affecting child development: "the quality of the relationships that children have with their parents"; "the relationships between the individuals who are raising the child"; and whether the family has "adequate economic resources" and "social and emotional supports."[43]

In his cross-examination of Lamb, attorney Terry Thompson made the following points: (1) many studies, including some that Lamb wrote, coauthored, or edited, emphasized the importance of fathers remaining in the family for the well-being of children, especially as role models for sons; (2) at least some of the studies emphasized the importance of biological parents for the well-being of children; and (3) none of the studies was based on a statistically random sample, and in many, if not all, cases the "control group" for a comparison of same-sex with heterosexual parents included some from the latter group who were not married, thus introducing another variable.[44] Lamb's responses, either directly to attorney Thompson or to attorney Matthew McGill on redirect, were: (1) his and others' studies on fathers were done in the 1970s and 1980s, and more recent data have called into question the importance of fathers and mothers, in contrast to two caring parents; (2) while conceding that the studies he reported on did not contain strict random samples, at least of a size adequate for confident generalization, he referred to a later study covering the entire universe of gay couples with children in the United States that reported results similar to those of the reported studies; and (3) it seemed to make sense to compare all heterosexual couples with children to all gay and lesbian couples with children.[45]

Attorney Thompson made every effort to show that political preferences accounted for the position that Lamb advocated. For example, he got Lamb to concede that at least part of a statement by the American Academy of Child and Adolescent Psychiatry was based on "non-scientific considerations."[46] On the claim that if gay and lesbian couples could marry, their children would be better off, Lamb acknowledged that no study looked at the quality of life of children raised by gay or lesbian couples in a domestic partnership.[47]

Leon Kass and Harvey Mansfield offered an alternative interpretation of current social science evidence on the question of family structure and child-rearing: the data were not yet extensive enough, in number or time, to allow for a scientifically significant conclusion.[48] Then the question became, which party had the burden of proof?[49] If the burden fell to defenders of traditional marriage, there would be risks, although it is hard to be certain of their extent. As Amy Wax pointed out in her law review article on the meaning of marriage, "The Conservative's Dilemma: Traditional Institutions, Social Change, and Same-Sex Marriage," conservatives do not want to risk losing the benefits of marriage as it exists in order to test what might happen to marriage if it were changed to include same-sex couples: "To satisfy social science standards, conservatives must come forward with data that systematically compares the effects of established arrangements with innovations they resist."[50] Professor Wax reports that Jonathan Rauch, a strong advocate of same-sex marriage, is aware that the long-term effects of such a change in the marriage laws are uncertain.[51]

Wax concluded her article by supporting another argument that Rauch put forward: as procreation and child-rearing are becoming less important and caregiving is becoming more important as people live longer, the differences between same-sex and opposite-sex couples are thus reduced in significance.[52] Such a point merits consideration. Wax did not say whether it would justify judicial action enforcing this change in marriage laws. One can infer that she would not oppose what happened in Vermont and New York. But I think her argument supports my contention that legislatures, not courts, should make that decision.

C. The Court of Appeals Decision: *Perry v. Brown*

When the governor of California declined to appeal the district court's decision in *Perry v. Schwarzenegger* invalidating Proposition 8, the proponents of the measure appealed to the Ninth Circuit Court of Appeals.[53] Judge Reinhardt wrote the circuit court opinion. After reciting the two bases for the district court's invalidation of Proposition 8—Due Process and Equal Protection—Judge Reinhardt presented a third position, one which the plaintiffs (and San Francisco, a plaintiff-intervenor) introduced:

> Proposition 8 singles out same-sex couples for unequal treatment by *taking away* from them alone the right to marry, and this action amounts to a distinct constitutional violation because the Equal Protection Clause protects minority groups from being targeted for the deprivation of an existing right without a legitimate reason.[54]

Such an approach, which relied on the U.S. Supreme Court's *Romer* decision, does not affirm an unqualified right of same-sex marriage and, consequently, only affected California. Judge N. R. Smith dissented on this point, arguing that Colorado's Amendment 2 can be distinguished from Proposition 8 in terms of its greater breadth.[55] Here is another difference: In the Colorado case, the constitutional referendum known as Amendment 2 rescinded state and local governmental acts of the legislative and executive branches.[56] In contrast, Proposition 8 repealed the decision of the California Supreme Court that went beyond what the U.S. Supreme Court had held the

U.S. Constitution to require, as well as what the people of California thought their constitution required.[57]

In his dissent, Judge Smith noted that, whereas the *Romer* Court concluded that "animus" accounted for Amendment 2, the California Supreme Court acknowledged reasons for the traditional marriage law apart from animus.[58] The proposition passed rational basis review, Judge Smith wrote, on the basis of the people's interest in responsible procreation and optimal parenting.[59] The plaintiffs argued and the California Supreme Court agreed that a law that excluded a class of persons from marriage did not advance these legitimate interests.[60] This objection applied to the second reason as well as the first because California did not prohibit same-sex couples from raising children. Judge Smith replied: "[I]t does not necessarily follow that the optimal parenting rationale is an *illegitimate* governmental interest."[61] To the plaintiffs' argument that Proposition 8 would have to change the laws regarding child-rearing in order to be rationally related to optimal parenting, Judge Smith replied, "this argument subjects Proposition 8 to heightened scrutiny review."[62] I think his argument would have been stronger had he asserted the people's right to govern via the popular constitutional referendum, which California provides.

The Ninth Circuit upheld the district court's invalidation of Proposition 8 in such a way as to limit the decision's reach to California and the few other states that might elect to move back from a decision for same-sex marriage, be it by legislative or judicial action.[63] Because the U.S. Supreme Court refused to decide the case on the merits, and because it did decide a related case that has a bearing on the main issue concerning same-sex marriage on the merits,[64] I want to discuss this successful legal challenge to the Defense of Marriage Act.

D. The Other Federal Case: Section 3 of DOMA

Congress passed DOMA in 1996.[65] Section 2 of DOMA guaranteed that states were not obliged to recognize same-sex marriages celebrated in other states.[66] But Congress also passed section 3, which reflected its refusal to recognize same-sex marriages for the purpose of federal benefits. Section 3 provided:

> In determining the meaning of any Act of Congress, or of any ruling, regulation, or interpretation of the various administrative bureaus and agencies of the United States, the word "marriage" means only a legal union between one man and one woman as husband and wife, and the word "spouse" refers only to a person of the opposite sex who is a husband or a wife.[67]

United States v. Windsor arose in November 2010, when Edith Windsor sought a refund on the federal estate tax (of $363,053) that she was required to pay as executor of the estate of her late spouse, Thea Spyer.[68] The two women lived together in New York City for over 40 years. In 2007, when Spyer became ill, they traveled to Canada to get married.[69] The marriage was recognized in New York before the state passed its own law enabling same-sex couples to marry.[70] Several months after the suit commenced, in February 2011, Attorney General Eric Holder announced that the Department of Justice would no longer defend section 3 of DOMA because the Attorney General and the President concluded "that a heightened standard of scrutiny should apply to classifications based on sexual orientation."[71] This was unusual in a double sense. First, the Justice Department was changing its mind about a law that it had initially considered constitutional—in the absence of any judicial decision invalidating the law. Second, it was deciding that heightened scrutiny applied to all laws concerning sexual orientation, even though neither the Supreme Court nor any other federal court had come to that conclusion.

The Justice Department's change of mind regarding the law's constitutionality did not require that broader conclusion. In the district court, Judge Barbara Jones, after citing the Supreme Court's *Cleburne* case for the reluctance of courts "to create new suspect classes," nonetheless held that section 3 of DOMA was unconstitutional as applied to the plaintiff.[72] She rejected arguments regarding the tradition of marriage, procreation, and childrearing as only indirectly affected by the law.[73]

DOMA did not define who *could* marry, and it did not say who could adopt and raise children.[74] Rather, in limiting the legal definition of "marriage" to a union between a man and woman, DOMA did not provide a federal incentive to same-sex couples.[75] A genuine desire for consistency would have required federal rules for age of consent and degree of consanguinity.[76]

In a divided opinion, the Second Circuit affirmed the decision of the district court. After reviewing the Supreme Court's discussion of the relevant considerations for determining when heightened scrutiny applies,[77] Judge Jacobs, writing for the court, held that "homosexuals compose a class that is subject to heightened scrutiny."[78]

E. In the Supreme Court: *Hollingsworth* and *Windsor* (2013)

The U.S. Supreme Court granted certiorari in both the Proposition 8 case and the Second Circuit's DOMA case on December 7, 2012 and handed down its decisions in both cases on June 26, 2013.[79] In *Hollingsworth*, which raised the fundamental constitutional question concerning same-sex marriage, the Court, in a 5-to-4 decision, held that the proponents of Proposition 8 lacked standing.[80] Chief Justice Roberts wrote that Petitioners could demonstrate no particularized injury from or interest in the outcome.[81] In *Windsor*, Justice Kennedy (who dissented in *Hollingsworth*) wrote the court opinion, holding that the Bipartisan Legal Advisory Group of the House of Representatives (BLAG) had standing to sue on behalf of Congress and that section 3 of DOMA violated the concept of equal protection as the Court has read it into the Fifth Amendment's Due Process Clause.[82] Justices Ginsburg, Breyer, Kagan, and Sotomayor joined the Court's opinion.[83] Justices Roberts, Scalia, and Alito wrote dissenting opinions in which they addressed the merits of the case as well as the standing question.[84]

Justice Kennedy tipped his hand when he noted that New York, along with other states, had decided that "[t]he limitation of lawful marriage to heterosexual couples" was "an unjust exclusion."[85] He then noted that marriage is primarily a state law matter, and, with very few and limited exceptions, the federal government accepts a state's marriage laws when it provides federal benefits for married couples or surviving spouses.[86] Then he shifted his emphasis from federalism to the substantive marriage issue: "The State's power in defining the marital relation is of central relevance in this case quite apart from principles of federalism."[87] The federal Defense of Marriage Act

> requires this Court now to address whether the resulting injury and indignity is a deprivation of an essential part of the liberty protected by the Fifth Amendment. What the State of New York treats as alike the federal law deems unlike by a law designed to injure the same class the State seeks to protect.[88]

Justice Kennedy referenced the House Report on DOMA, which expressed moral disapproval of homosexuality, and concluded: "[I]nterference with the equal dignity of same-sex marriages, a dignity conferred by the States in the exercise of their sovereign power, was more than an incidental effect of the federal statute."[89] DOMA "places same-sex couples in an unstable position of being in a second-tier marriage. The differentiation demeans the couple, whose moral and sexual choices the Constitution protects, and whose relationship the State has sought to dignify."[90] Thus, the Court held, "DOMA is unconstitutional as a deprivation of the liberty of the person protected by the Fifth Amendment of the Constitution."[91]

Suppose another state refused to recognize a same-sex marriage performed in New York? Section 2 of DOMA expressly protected each state's right to decide such questions.[92] While Justice Kennedy made no reference to section 2 of DOMA, his discussion of the harm of taking away the "dignity" that marriage confers[93] led several lower federal courts to conclude that such non-recognition was unconstitutional.[94]

The three dissenting opinions treat the merits question in distinctive ways, although each justice disagreed with the majority's characterization of DOMA as intending to injure or harm same-sex couples. Justice Scalia's opinion, which Justice Thomas joined, restated what he wrote in his *Lawrence* dissent: "[T]he Constitution does not forbid the government to enforce traditional moral and sexual norms," and it "neither requires nor forbids our society to approve of same-sex marriage."[95] Justice Alito contrasted the traditional definition of marriage, which he called "conjugal," with the newer view, which he called "consent-based," and concluded that the Constitution does not require one or the other, while the Court's *Windsor* decision implicitly endorsed the consent-based view of marriage.[96] Chief Justice Roberts's brief dissent took one paragraph to disagree with the majority's contention that DOMA's " 'principal purpose' . . . was a bare desire to harm."[97] He was much more interested in confining the reach of the court opinion to this case, lest any of Justice Kennedy's statements suggest that the Court would come to a comparable decision in a future case contesting a state's traditional marriage law.[98] He quoted what Justice Kennedy said at the very end of his opinion, that "[t]his opinion and its holding are confined to those lawful marriages" which states allowing same-sex marriage have already chosen to recognize.[99]

Chief Justice Roberts disagreed with Justice Scalia's description of this part of the Court's opinion as a "bald, unreasoned disclaime[r]."[100] Rather he stressed that this "disclaimer is a logical and necessary consequence of the argument the majority has chosen to adopt."[101] Where Chief Justice Roberts wanted to emphasize the federalism aspect of the Court's opinion, Justice Scalia seems to have concluded, with even more conviction than when he wrote his *Lawrence* dissent, that Justice Kennedy had already decided that the Constitution required all states to recognize same-sex marriage and, as a result, that the Court would make that decision in the next case to raise the issue that came before it. Justice Scalia spelled that out by quoting three distinct passages from the Court's opinion and by pointing out how little needed to be changed to use the same argument to strike down a state's limitation on marriage to the union of a man and a woman.[102]

F. After *Hollingsworth* and *Windsor*: From the Lower Federal Courts Back to the Supreme Court

That Justice Scalia's assumption proved correct does not mean that Justice Kennedy had truly made up his mind on the underlying same-sex marriage question when he wrote his *Windsor* opinion for the court.[103] He may well have expected to have the benefit of other judicial rulings on the question in light of the Court's *Windsor* decision. Still, after *Windsor*, the lower courts delivered a resounding affirmation of the right to same-sex marriage. From June 2013 to June 2015, 30 federal courts in 48 cases and 15 state courts in 17 cases invalidated bans on same-sex marriage.[104] Five different U.S. circuit courts heard appeals in same-sex marriage cases. The first four decisions agreed with virtually all of the district courts that the federal Constitution required same-sex marriage.[105] Then the Sixth Circuit reversed the district courts in the six cases arising out of states under its jurisdiction.[106] That decision, in November 2014, created a division among the circuits, which led the Supreme Court to hear the same-sex marriage case again; the Court granted certiorari in three of the Sixth Circuit cases on January 16, 2015. Prior to the Sixth Circuit's decision, all of the district and circuit court opinions relied on the Supreme Court's *Windsor* decision to set aside the Court's earlier dismissal of a challenge to Minnesota's traditional marriage law[107] and then proceeded to use the Court's fundamental right to marry cases, starting with *Loving*, to establish strict scrutiny as the standard for examining bans on same-sex marriage. From there, the outcome was obvious, because any argument justifying the limitation of marriage to opposite-sex couples that relied on procreation and raising children was subject to a finding that it was both over- and under-inclusive. Many heterosexual couples did not and/or would not have children, and some same-sex couples did have children, or wanted to, via adoption or artificial reproduction.

Aware of the Court's longstanding admonition to "go slow" with the introduction of new "fundamental rights,"[108] the majority opinions labored to demonstrate that a new right was not being created, that the cases which gave rise to the right to marry viewed the right generally, not with respect to a specific group of individuals. The central question was whether striking down anti-miscegenation laws implied that the traditional understanding that marriage consisted in the union of a man and a woman was no longer valid. I think a more candid explanation for these lower court decisions comes from district court Judge Shelby in the *Kitchen* case. Quoting from Justice Kennedy's *Lawrence* opinion to the effect that "times can blind us to certain truths" and that "every generation can invoke [the Constitution's] principles in their own search for greater freedom,"[109] he went on to say:

> Here it is not the Constitution that has changed, but the knowledge of what it means to be gay or lesbian. The court cannot ignore the fact that the Plaintiffs are able to develop a committed intimate relationship with a person of the same sex but not with a person of the opposite sex. The court, and the State, must adapt to this changed understanding."[110]

Accepting what Judge Shelby says about intimate homosexual relationships, the question remains whether the initiative for "adapt[ing] to this changed understanding," and thereby changing the definition of marriage, lies with the courts or with the people through their popularly elected legislatures. To apply strict scrutiny analysis is to turn judges into the government officials who decide what the best policy is. The effect of such scrutiny, and more generally the approach that almost every judge took to the same-sex marriage controversy after the Supreme Court's *Windsor* decision, has been to refuse to acknowledge any merit in a legislative determination to retain a state's traditional marriage laws.

The Seventh and Ninth Circuit courts subjected the traditional marriage laws to heightened scrutiny after holding that laws classifying by sexual orientation required it.[111] Judge Richard Posner wrote the court opinion for the Seventh Circuit. He emphasized that the two cases before him "are about the welfare of American children." He confidently asserted that the case required heightened scrutiny because refusing to authorize or recognize such marriages is discrimination against a class that is defined by "an immutable (and probably an innate, in the sense of in-born) characteristic rather than a choice."[112]

Later in his opinion, Judge Posner described with approval John Stuart Mill's view of the harms that government may properly address, thereby implying that the U.S. Constitution embodies Mill's principle. "The harm must be tangible, secular, material—physical or financial, or, if emotional, focused and direct—rather than moral or spiritual."[113] Judge Posner claims to stop short of reading Mill into the Constitution: "Though these decisions [*Loving* and *Lawrence*] are in the spirit of Mill, Mill is not the last word on public morality."[114] Still, the argument against the state's traditional marriage laws emphasizes the immediate harms, material and psychological, to same-sex couples, especially those with children, and the speculative character of the possible future harm to what might be an increasing number of children who will not know their biological parents.[115]

Judge Stephen Reinhardt wrote the opinion for the Ninth Circuit. He cited a previous Ninth Circuit decision that interpreted the Supreme Court's *Windsor* decision to establish heightened scrutiny for classifications based on sexual orientation.[116] And he had no difficulty rejecting arguments based on the desirability of having children raised by two parents of the opposite sex, concluding that they lacked adequate support.[117]

The unanimous Ninth Circuit panel covered all the arguments for same-sex marriage. Judge Reinhardt also wrote a separate concurring opinion making the case that the Supreme Court's fundamental right to marry cases encompassed same-sex marriage. Judge Berzon wrote a concurrence arguing that the prohibition on same-sex marriage was a form of sex discrimination.

On November 6, 2014, the Sixth Circuit handed down a 2-to-1 decision reversing the district courts and upholding the bans on same-sex marriage in Michigan, Kentucky, Ohio, and Tennessee. Judge Jeffrey Sutton's court opinion in *DeBoer v. Snyder*[118] contrasts with the opinions in the other four circuits by emphasizing the democratic process of government over the "rights" question and by examining the constitutional question in terms of rational basis scrutiny.

Judge Sutton began by noting "this is a case about change—and how best to handle it under the United States Constitution," and "the question is not whether American law will allow gay couples to marry; it is when and how that will happen," as a result of legislative, initiative based, or judicial decisions that permit or require same-sex marriage. Judge Sutton made his case for deferring to the legislatures in this way:

> Process and structure matter greatly in American government. Indeed, they may be the most reliable, liberty assuring guarantees of our system of government, requiring us to take seriously the route the United States Constitution contemplates for making such a fundamental change to such a fundamental social condition.[119]

While no judge would disagree about the importance of process and structure in American government, judges supporting same-sex marriage often cited the Supreme Court's flag salute case to affirm the principle that "fundamental rights may not be submitted to vote; they depend on the outcome of no elections."[120] For her part, dissenting Judge Martha Craig Daughtrey asserted that the majority's "who should decide?" approach "leads us through a largely irrelevant discourse on democracy and federalism. In point of fact, the real issue before us concerns what is at stake in these six cases for the individual plaintiffs and their children, and what should be done about it."[121]

Judge Daughtrey agreed with the other four circuits. She concluded that the fundamental right to marry included same-sex couples and that the ban on same-sex marriage violated the Equal Protection Clause because classifications based on sexual orientation were, by implication after *Windsor*, subject to heightened scrutiny. In addition, Judge Daughtrey suggested that animus against homosexuals could be inferred from a state's failure to allow same-sex couples to marry.[122]

Judge Sutton, on the other hand, interpreted the precedents narrowly on both counts: the fundamental right to marry arose in cases in which marriage was understood to involve a man and a woman, and the Supreme Court had not yet held sexual orientation subject to "heightened scrutiny." He also thought that a legislature could reasonably decide the issue either way without being charged with hostility to gays.

The difference between the two sides, in this and in the other circuit court cases, on the significance of the fundamental right to marry seems to turn on how one assesses other changes in marriage laws in relation to the substitution of "two persons" for "a man and a woman." Judge Daughtrey quotes from a law review article which describes marriage "historically" as "a profoundly unequal institution," in which the woman had no independent legal existence; she was regarded as property of her husband; "it was legally impossible for a man to rape his wife;" and "dissolving the marital partnership via divorce was exceedingly difficult."[123] Judge Daughtrey presents this material in response to Justice Alito's suggestion, in his *Windsor* dissent, that opponents of DOMA were introducing an expanded definition of marriage. For Judge Daughtrey, marriage laws are in constant evolution and, in general, that's a good thing because the changes have made the relationship more just. Even if that is true, and some would contest that "no fault divorce" has been an unqualified improvement, the changes identified do not seem to be of the same magnitude as a change that eliminates the male-female component and its connection to having and raising children.

Judge Sutton's approach to changes in marriage law reflected his conservative approach to constitutional interpretation:

The theory of the living constitution rests on the premise that every generation has the right to govern itself. If that premise prevents judges from insisting on principles that society has moved past, so too should it prevent judges from anticipating principles that society has yet to embrace.[124]

Judge Daughtrey rejected that approach, quoting Judge Posner's contention that it is "so full of holes that it cannot be taken seriously."[125] Judge Posner was referring to the lack of evidence to show that children are better off raised by opposite-sex couples, as well as the over- and under-inclusive nature of laws that place no requirements on opposite-sex couples, regarding procreation, and allow no same-sex couples to marry, even if they are raising children. Of course, putting the burden of proof on the defenders of the traditional understanding of marriage to justify the non-expansion of marriage is what characterizes "strict" or "heightened" scrutiny, and the position of Judge Sutton and the other judges who refused to require same-sex marriage was that under the proper, rational basis standard the traditional marriage laws should be upheld.

Judge Daughtrey's response to this position, which included an explanation for why she would apply heightened scrutiny in these cases, inferred from the absence of a willingness to change the marriage law animus toward homosexuals.

[T]he Supreme Court has instructed [us] that an exclusionary law violates the Equal Protection Clause when it is based not upon relevant facts, but instead upon only a general, ephemeral distrust of, or discomfort with, a particular group, for example when legislation is justified by the bare desire to exclude an unpopular group from a social institution or arrangement.[126]

G. Summary: How Things Stood as the U.S. Supreme Court Prepared to Hear Oral Argument in *Obergefell*

The near unanimity of support in the federal courts and in the state courts in 2014 for advocates of same-sex marriage stands in contrast to the closely divided results in the highest state courts from 1993 to 2009.[127] Clearly, the previous Supreme Court decision on same-sex marriage, *Baker v. Nelson*, in which the Court dismissed the case for failure to raise a substantial federal question,[128] had been superseded by the Court's decisions on sex and sexual orientation classifications.[129] The other main reason for the shift in outcomes has to be the Court's *Windsor* decision, in particular, parts of Justice Kennedy's majority opinion, as well as Justice Scalia's dissent.

The Court's *Windsor* opinion emphasized the "dignity" that the right to marry accords couples, and the ensuing harm that results from taking away that status.[130] Hence that argument could easily be extended to cover a state's refusal to deny this "fundamental right" to same-sex couples, including those who were married in another jurisdiction, whether in another state or in Canada, as well as those who wish to marry in their own state. In striking down section 3 of DOMA, the *Windsor* Court said nothing about section two,[131] which guarantees each state the right to determine its own marriage laws regardless of what other states do.[132] Nor did any of the lower federal court opinions discuss that question.[133]

If *Windsor* had been read as a federalism case, section 2 of DOMA could have remained good law, and if a state's public policy opposed such marriages, that position should have been held constitutional. But since *Windsor* was interpreted to include a substantive due process conception of "dignity," the difference between federal non-recognition of such marriages and a state's non-recognition seems slight. And if a state has to recognize marriages performed in other states, how can it justify not allowing such marriages in its own jurisdiction?

The lower federal courts grappled with the same constitutional issues that the state high courts did. The main constitutional arguments concerned, on the one hand, the Due Process Clause and the cases establishing marriage as a fundamental right and, on the other hand, the Equal Protection Clause and the level of scrutiny to be accorded a classification by sexual orientation.[134] The due process issue required judges to decide whether the Court's understanding of the fundamental right to marry could legitimately be applied to this new context of same-sex couples. For example, the Tenth and Fourth Circuits came to that conclusion and then had an easy time demonstrating that the state's interests in supporting procreation and the raising of children were not narrowly tailored to the exclusion of same-sex couples from marriage.[135] The Seventh and Ninth Circuits concluded that either *Windsor* or other cases had effectively made sexual orientation a quasi-suspect classification, with the result that traditional marriage laws, often affirmed by constitutional bans on same-sex marriage, would be subject to heightened scrutiny. Either form of heightened scrutiny results in a constitutional decision requiring same-sex marriage.

For almost all of the lower federal court judges,[136] the combination of judicial recognition of the "normalcy" of homosexuality (reflected in *Lawrence*) and the emphasis on the dignity that marriage imparts has yielded the conclusion that sexual orientation is virtually as irrelevant to legitimate government action as is race. This goes against the Supreme Court's more conservative approach to fundamental rights as stated in *Washington v. Glucksberg*.[137] The emphasis on what was deeply rooted in the country's history and tradition seems to be trumped by a conviction held by most lower federal court judges that extending the right to marry to same-sex couples has no harmful effects, either on heterosexuals, who will continue to marry and raise and care for their children, or on children raised by same-sex couples, and therefore should be granted.

After the *Windsor* decision, the judgments of the lower federal courts and the state courts had been almost unanimously for "marriage equality." For the opponents of same-sex marriage to prevail in the Supreme Court, they would have to emphasize judicial restraint rather than to make a positive argument for the traditional definition of marriage. Such a limitation put defenders of traditional marriage at a disadvantage.

CHAPTER SEVEN

The Supreme Court Settles the Matter

Marriage as a Fundamental Right

ON JANUARY 16, 2015, THE SUPREME COURT GRANTED THE CER-
tiorari petition in the cluster of same-sex marriage cases that came
from the Sixth Circuit.[1] The Court consolidated the cases and asked
the parties to address two questions in two different periods of oral
argument, both scheduled for April 28 of that year.

For Question 1, "Does the Fourteenth Amendment require a
state to license a marriage between two people of the same sex?" the
Court allotted ninety minutes.

Question 2, "Does the Fourteenth Amendment require a state
to recognize a marriage between two people of the same sex when
their marriage was lawfully licensed and performed out of state?"
was allotted sixty minutes.[2]

Because the Court decided the first question in the affirmative,
it did not hand down a decision in the second. Therefore I limit
my discussion to the briefs and oral argument concerning the first
question.

The Briefs

Petitioners' brief in *DeBoer v. Snyder*[3] began with the Equal Protection Clause argument. They asserted that Michigan's marriage
amendment and related statutes could not survive "even rational

basis review."[4] Petitioners presented the rational basis test as requiring the State to show a legitimate legislative purpose, not one that is based on "prejudice, fear, animus, or moral disapproval of a particular group," and that the means chosen, in the form of legislation, be "logically and plausibly related to the legitimate purpose."[5] Applying the test, Petitioners characterized traditional marriage laws as "target[ing] an historically unpopular minority" by "disqualify[ing] an entire swath of citizens from a civil institution of fundamental societal importance—with highly stigmatizing consequences."[6] As a result, Petitioners contended that the state's main constitutional defense addressed the wrong question: "While the State seeks to discuss why it *includes* different-sex couples in marriage, the proper question is why it *excludes* same-sex couples from marriage."[7]

The difficulty with this argument, I believe, is that it elides the undisputed history of discrimination against homosexuals with the institution of marriage, which has always consisted in the union of a man and a woman with a view toward procreation and raising children. Petitioners argued that a state's failure to change its marriage laws to include homosexuals, in light of society's changed understanding of homosexuality and the desire of some same-sex couples to marry, reflected purposeful discrimination. As Petitioners put it, "the primary purpose and practical effect of Michigan's marriage bans [is] to demean same-sex couples and their families."[8] Petitioners claimed that "the impermissibility" of the statutory and constitutional bans was demonstrated "by both their text and the context," since they were enacted when some states were granting same-sex couples the right to marry.[9] As Respondents pointed out, the constitutional amendment provision, which does remove the issue from the ordinary political process, was deemed necessary due to the robust judicial action by state supreme courts.[10] Of course it would have been preferable if other states had followed Hawaii and passed a constitutional amendment affirming that the issue of same-sex marriage was for the legislature to decide. But a political response to a fear that judicial action would remove the matter from the state's political process cannot undeniably be characterized as purposeful discrimination. It could just as well be motivated by a desire to protect its political process against judicial overreaching. This exchange between the parties highlights the role which the forum—legislature or judiciary—played in the same-sex controversy, although that role was not often discussed.

Respondents' brief emphasized the "liberty to engage in self-government,"[11] and the limited requirements of rational basis review.[12] To illustrate the first point, Respondents noted that the issue was being debated in the several states, and while eleven states had decided to enact same-sex marriage through the political process, courts settled the matter by requiring same-sex marriage in twenty-six other states.[13] Both sides of the *Obergefell* Court took note of this action. The majority noted that the issue had been fully vetted, putting political and judicial action together.[14] The dissent made the point Respondents' counsel made: the Court's decision terminated an appropriate form of the political process.[15] The Solicitor General, addressing this point in his oral argument, described the results of the political process as reflecting a house divided, suggesting that whatever value federalism had, it should not result in same-sex marriage in some states but not in others.[16] From Respondents' perspective, as well as that of four justices, "marriage's definition is not a legal issue; it is a public policy issue."[17]

Respondents' argument in support of the state's traditional marriage law emphasized the "biological complementarity"[18] of male and female, which can give rise to procreation. Not "animus toward individuals outside that rubric," but the relationship between "procreation[] and the raising of children"[19] accounted for the state's interest in marriage.

But what would happen if same-sex couples could marry? Respondents' first reply was that "separating marriage from procreation dramatically changes the state's interest in the institution,"[20] which raises a question as to why the state would be interested in providing public benefits for marriage. One could point to the plaintiffs in this case, two women who are nurses, each of whom has adopted a handicapped child and wished to receive the recognition and benefits of marriage.[21]

Respondents also suggested that Michigan values the contributions of fathers and mothers to parenting, and that "changing the definition of marriage to remove its inherent connection to procreation might undermine it in the long term as an institution for linking parents to their biological children."[22] Respondents replied to Petitioners' contention that Michigan marriage laws reflect animus toward same-sex couples by saying that its interest lies in "the benefits to a child in having a close connection to the biological mother and biological father when possible."[23]

This response prompts us to keep in mind the standard for rational basis review, and how close a "fit" is necessary to satisfy that standard. Is it enough to simply present the reason for what is included without giving any explanation for exclusion, even if the exclusion is fairly described as a "non-inclusion"? After all, same-sex marriage has only recently become a matter of public policy deliberation. In advancing its position that no explanation is necessary, Respondents cited *Heller v. Doe*, a case which concerned involuntary commitment and two different standards of proof for mental retardation and mental illness. In upholding the state law in that case, the Court explained that rational basis review, which it was applying, did not require the state "to produce evidence to sustain the rationality of a statutory classification."[24] The *Heller* Court had also noted that rational basis review "is accorded a strong presumption of validity" for "a classification neither involving fundamental rights nor proceeding along suspect lines. . . ."[25] If a state's decision to retain restrictive marriage laws is not by itself regarded as discriminatory against homosexuals, and if rational basis review, understood even as Gunther suggests "with bite," is applied, does the Constitution's Equal Protection Clause require a change in marriage laws to include same-sex couples?

In their reply brief, Petitioners argued: "The bans withhold from same-sex families legal protections for their intimacy and autonomy."[26] Legal protections could have been provided the way Vermont did originally, with civil unions legislation, which is similar to what California's legislature provided on their own initiative.[27] But Petitioners would not have been satisfied with that, given the emphasis they placed on dignity, which only marriage would confer. As for Respondents' contention that Michigan's laws reflected a preference for biological complementarity and were not per se classifications based on sexual orientation, Petitioners contended "that is just another way of describing the fact that the laws do not allow same-sex couples to wed. . . ."[28] That is true, but the emphasis on biological complementarity suggests a positive reason for defining marriage as the union of a man and a woman, whereas the emphasis on the characteristics of the excluded class implies a discriminatory intent.

The Justice Department's amicus brief limited itself to reasserting its view, first stated in the *Windsor* case, that classification by sexual orientation should be subject to heightened scrutiny. While its focus was on the Equal Protection Clause, and its brief did not venture an opinion on the fundamental right to marry under the Due Process Clause, its argument emphasized the importance of marriage and the fact that lesbian and gay couples numbered "more than 700,000 families, including nearly 220,000 children."[29]

This information forms the basis of a part of the argument that a majority of the Supreme Court accepted: that numerous same-sex couples lived in committed relationships similar to opposite-sex couples, and a substantial minority were also raising children.

The Justice Department pressed the position that, based on the Court's precedents, sexual orientation should be subject to heightened scrutiny. These factors were: (1) the class had suffered a history of discrimination; (2) the characteristic that prompted the discrimination frequently bore no relation to the ability to perform or contribute to society; (3) the discrimination was based on an immutable characteristic which defined the discrete group; and (4) the class was a politically powerless minority.[30]

Since the Court has shied away from expanding the category of "suspect" or "quasi-suspect" classifications, at the same time that it has decided cases in favor of gay rights, and since it continued to do so in *Obergefell*, we need not go into a detailed examination of these four factors and how they might apply in this case. The most interesting difference of opinion arises in connection with the first point, the history of discrimination. The government acknowledged that marriage laws were not written to discriminate against homosexuals, but it contended that heightened scrutiny applied across the board once it was determined that a class has been subject to discrimination and satisfied the rest of the test. The Court's approach to race-based affirmative action was offered as an example.[31]

Apart from the question whether the Court has truly followed strict scrutiny in its affirmative action cases,[32] the justices themselves seemed to have doubts about their ability to distinguish in a principled way the application of the three distinct levels of scrutiny.[33] I think that accounts for the Court's refusal to expand the category of "suspect" classifications, even while it takes a careful look at governmental classifications, including sexual orientation. The Court surely took a careful look under rational basis scrutiny in *Romer v. Evans* and *Lawrence v. Texas*. But isn't the issue of same-sex marriage different from the issue of criminalizing the only form of sexual activity that homosexuals can engage in? The consequence of any form of heightened scrutiny is a judicial requirement for a near perfect act of legislation. The "fit" between the end sought and the means chosen must be so good that there is little if any over-inclusion and under-inclusion. Hence traditional marriage laws would fail the test, since the state's interest in having children raised in stable families is not satisfied by opposite-sex couples who do not have children and yet may marry, and it is satisfied by same-sex couples who are not allowed to marry, but are nevertheless raising children. But is such a constitutional requirement appropriate? It does not give the legislatures much leeway. The argument for heightened scrutiny is based on the assumption that some form of discrimination is "afoot" with certain classifications.[34] Is this assumption valid where traditional marriage laws are challenged?

Oral Argument

The ninety minutes allotted for oral argument on whether the Fourteenth Amendment required a state to allow two people of the same sex to marry was divided equally among the attorneys, for the Petitioners, the Respondents, and the United States.

While oral argument may or may not make a difference in the outcome of a Supreme Court case, the questions the justices put to the attorneys suggest how they understand the issues, or they may ask a question as a means of carrying on a unstated dialog with another justice. The justices's questioning during oral argument revealed the two distinct positions that came out in the Court's 5-to-4 decision and its majority and dissenting opinions.

Mary Bonauto, attorney for Petitioners, began by describing the ban on same-sex marriage as putting "the stain of unworthiness" on gay people as a class in violation of "the basic constitutional commitment to equal dignity."[35] Responding to Justice Ginsburg's question about deference to state government decisions, Ms. Bonauto referred to the *Windsor* decision and added that here "a whole class of people" were denied "the equal right to be able to join in this very extensive government institution that provides protection for families."[36] This prompted Chief Justice Roberts to point out that the Respondents' position was that the institution, understood as the union of a man and a woman in the United States and in most other places until the Massachusetts decision in 2003, was being redefined by the Petitioners and hence changed. Ms. Bonauto countered that the institution had constantly been in evolution, and in the direction of equality. Justice Ginsburg subsequently supported this position by referring to ancient "coverture" laws, by which married women's legal interests were covered by their husbands.[37] Then Justice Kennedy, whom both parties knew was the likely swing vote, asked about Respondents' argument concerning time to work out the proper resolution.[38] Ms. Bonauto referred to a twenty-year period from the Hawaii case as evidence that the American people had been debating gay marriage.[39] Justice Alito then asked Ms. Bonauto whether, based on Petitioners' brief, she thought that the primary purpose of Michigan's marriage law was "to demean gay people."[40] Ms. Bonauto replied first that such laws "encompass moral judgments and stereotypes about gay people."[41] And when Justice Alito said that marriage had until recently been understood as the union of a man and a woman, Ms. Bonauto replied with a phrase from Justice Kennedy at the end of his *Lawrence* opinion: "Your honor, my position is that times can blind."[42] She elaborated with reference to the Fourteenth Amendment and the Supreme Court's increased scrutiny of sex classifications in the 1970s, and finally the gay rights cases of *Romer, Lawrence,* and *Windsor.*[43] At that point Justice Ginsburg rejoined the discussion with reflections on the evolution of marriage law toward equality.[44]

Justice Breyer's questions on this subject, first to Ms. Bonauto and then to John Bursch, attorney for Respondents, illustrate the significance of how the marriage issue is understood: should the focus be on who is *included* or who is *excluded*? Justice Breyer asked Ms. Bonauto to explain why "nine people outside the ballot box" should require states to change their marriage laws.[45] In response, she cited the Fourteenth Amendment and the *Loving* case, which invalidated anti-miscegenation laws.[46] Justice Breyer was apparently satisfied; he did not reply, as he could have, by noting the distinction between the relevance of sexual difference for procreation and the irrelevance of race similarity for that purpose. He came back to the same question with Mr. Bursch, however, indicating as his presupposition that there was a fundamental liberty interest in marriage and that the burden was on the Respondents to justify the exclusion of gays from that institution.[47] Justices Sotomayor and Kagan took precisely the same position on this issue. When you add Justice Kennedy to the four liberal justices—Ginsburg, Breyer, Sotomayor and Kagan—that makes five votes for putting the burden on the Respondents. And Mr. Bursch made no headway with the argument that delinking procreation from marriage, by allowing same-sex couples to marry, would have a negative effect on the permanence of heterosexual marriages.[48] Justice Sotomayor dismissed such a position as a mere "feeling."[49]

On the other side, Justice Scalia took the position that, under rational basis analysis, the state was under no obligation to demonstrate the likelihood of its apprehensions regarding negative consequences from such a change in marriage laws.[50]

The only other potentially significant question came from the Chief Justice, who asked Mr. Bursch whether the marriage law he was defending could be described as discrimination by sex.[51] That was a surprising question coming from the Chief Justice. Was he truly considering this as a basis for requiring same-sex marriage, or did he simply want to get the reply on record lest one of the other justices made this argument? Mr. Bursch replied that all the precedents have "involved treating classes of men and women differently," and he then cited a case in which the Court upheld a law that involved citizenship claims based on the citizenship of a parent; the citizen father would have to prove paternity whereas the citizen mother would not.[52]

Justice Scalia also asked questions about how religious freedom claims could be recognized if the Court decided in favor of the Petitioners. Justices Sotomayor and Kagan were confident that proper distinctions could be drawn between government officials and religious officials and perhaps also official duties versus commercial activities.[53] When the same question was put to U.S. Solicitor General Donald Verrilli, he acknowledged that there could be some tough cases, such as a university that gets federal funding and offers married student housing but does not want to recognize same-sex marriages.[54] Also, a state with a civil rights act protecting against discrimination by sexual orientation might require merchants to offer their services to everyone. But those kinds of questions, he concluded, were surely not going to determine the outcome of this case.

The Supreme Court's Decision in *Obergefell v. Hodges*

On June 26, the Supreme Court handed down its decision. Justice Kennedy's court opinion, which I discussed briefly in the introduction, presented a conception of freedom that he first offered in his part of the joint opinion in the 1992 case on abortion *Planned Parenthood v. Casey* and developed in three gay rights cases: *Romer v. Evans* (1996), *Lawrence v. Texas* (2003), and *United States v. Windsor* (2013). The common elements of these opinions are an emphasis on liberty as autonomy and the absence of any discussion of levels of scrutiny.

Justice Kennedy's opinion begins with, and emphasizes, the fundamental right to marry, which comes under the Due Process Clause of the Fourteenth Amendment (as well as the Fifth).[55] The opinion also addresses the Equal Protection Clause argument with a view toward showing how the two clauses occasionally complement each other.

Because the right of same-sex couples to marry implicates liberty and equality claims, what is the difference between a constitutional argument based on "substantive due process" on the one hand and equal protection of the laws on the other? First, if the issue is treated under the Due Process Clause, the Court must confront the question whether its precedents on the fundamental right to marry apply to this new context. And if so, the Court is confronted with its *Glucksberg* precedent, according to which non-enumerated substantive rights must have the support of history and tradition.[56] If the Court assimilates same-sex marriage to the existing right, strict scrutiny would follow. While the Court did treat the issue in terms of the existing right, nowhere in Justice Kennedy's opinion did he mention the level of scrutiny he was applying. If, on the other hand, the Court had focused on the equal protection challenge, it might have felt obliged to take up the government's invitation to rule that classification by sexual orientation was inherently "suspect," and subject to heightened scrutiny. The outcome might have hinged on which level of scrutiny the Court chose to adopt. Since, however, the Court had conspicuously avoided a discussion of levels of scrutiny in its sexual orientation cases, starting with *Romer*,[57] we may assume that it preferred to look directly at the constitutional issue rather than to begin with the abstract categories. But the question concerning the proper amount of deference the Court should accord to the legislature remains.

I think the Court's preference for leading with marriage as a fundamental right reflects Justice Kennedy's continuing interest in reading the concepts of autonomy and dignity into the Constitution. This puts the focus on the individual claims on government, in terms of recognition and material benefits, rather than a consideration of how marriage laws include and exclude people in terms of community benefits and drawbacks. Justice Kennedy's reasoning for placing the claim of same-sex couples within the fundamental right to marry draws on the "equal protection" position when it refers to the number of same-sex couples that are raising children. While Chief Justice Roberts, in dissent, does a good job of calling into question the legitimacy of the Court's treatment of the fundamental right to marry, he does not specifically address the fact that same-sex couples with children—in many cases children who are adopted and thereby given a home—resemble opposite-sex couples with children but receive no recognition and no benefits. And no justice, or lower circuit court, considered the Vermont solution of civil unions, which involved recognition and all state benefits.

Justice Kennedy's opening paragraph, which I quoted in my introduction, highlights liberty as autonomy.

The Constitution promises liberty to all within its reach, a liberty that includes certain specific rights that allow persons, within a lawful realm, to define and express their identity.[58]

Contrast this passage from the Court's opinion in *Washington v. Glucksberg*, part of which Chief Justice Roberts quoted in his dissent:

[W]e "have always been reluctant to expand the concept of substantive due process because guideposts for responsible decision-making in this uncharted area are scarce and open-ended . . ." We must therefore "exercise the utmost care whenever we are asked to break new ground in this field," lest the liberty protected by the Due Process Clause be subtly transformed into the policy preferences of the members of this Court.[59]

Justice Kennedy's account of the history of marriage is meant to explain why *Obergefell* involves a right different from the one the Court treated in *Glucksberg* and why same-sex couples must also enjoy the right.[60] The difference between the majority opinion and the dissent comes out in their different treatments of Cicero's account of marriage in his treatise *De Officiis* (*On Duties*). Chief Justice Roberts, in order to demonstrate that the historical purpose of marriage pertained to having and raising children, quoted the first sentence of section 54.

> For since the reproductive instinct is by nature's gift the common possession of all living creatures, the first bond of union is that between husband and wife; the next, that between parents and children; then we find one home, with everything in common.[61]

Justice Kennedy, who cited the same edition and section, used Cicero to support his contention concerning "the centrality of marriage to the human condition," but he omitted Cicero's reference to the natural reproductive instinct in order to play down the traditional understanding of marriage.

> Confucius taught that marriage lies at the foundation of government [citation omitted]. This wisdom was echoed centuries later and half a world away by Cicero, who wrote, "The first bond of society is marriage; next children; and then the family."[62]

This illustrates the majority's decision to play down the significance of the change in marriage laws. By treating the expansion of marriage—from the union of a man and a woman to the union of two persons—as on a par with emancipating women from coverture laws and invalidating anti-miscegenation laws, Justice Kennedy can argue that the right of same-sex couples to marry follows from the Court's precedents on marriage.

Acknowledging Respondents' contention that marriage has historically involved a man and a woman, Justice Kennedy responded on behalf of Petitioners: "Were their intent to demean the revered idea and reality of marriage, the Petitioners' claims would be of a different order. But that is neither their purpose nor their submission."[63]

Justice Kennedy could have added, based on the briefs in the case and the oral argument, that satisfying the Petitioners' request did not appear to harm marriage as an institution.

After reviewing Supreme Court precedents on gay rights and taking note of the case law on the marriage question, including decisions from five appellate courts and numerous state high courts, and further taking note of legislation and referenda on the subject, Justice Kennedy indicated that the Court was prepared to make a decision. Before explaining the details of his reasoning, he offered these remarks to address the decision's break with tradition:

> The nature of injustice is that we may not always see it in our own times. The generations that wrote and ratified the Bill of Rights and the Fourteenth Amendment did not presume to know the extent of freedom in all of its dimensions, and so they entrusted to future generations a charter protecting the right of all persons to enjoy liberty as we learn its meaning. When new insight reveals discord between the Constitution's central protections and a received legal stricture, a claim to liberty must be addressed.[64]

The not-so-hidden implication of this statement, which both Justices Roberts and Scalia saw and criticized, is that the Court will use the general language of the Constitution, especially concerning the Due Process and Equal Protection Clauses, to eradicate injustice wherever it may be found in American government. Gone from such a formulation is any recognition that the political branches of government might have some responsibility for dealing with injustice or that, according to the principles of American government, the just powers of government, as spoken of in the Declaration of Independence, are derived from the consent of the governed.[65] Hence the very meaning of justice under the American Constitution requires a reconciliation of rights and consent.

Justice Kennedy then presented a four-part analysis to explain the Court's holding that states may not exclude same-sex couples from marrying. First, "the right to personal choice regarding marriage is inherent in the concept of individual autonomy."[66] Second, "the right to marry is fundamental because it supports a two-person union unlike any other in its importance to the committed individuals."[67] Third, the right to marry "safeguards children and families and thus draws meaning from related rights of childrearing, procreation, and education."[68] Fourth, "this Court's cases and the Nation's traditions make clear that marriage is a keystone of our social order."[69]

The first point confirms the importance Justice Kennedy attached to individual autonomy as a constitutionally protected liberty.[70] The second point redefined the essence of marriage, from a male-female union to any two-person union. This replies to suggestions from Justice Alito that allowing same-sex marriage would open the way to allowing plural marriages. The third point, by referring to childrearing, highlights the kind of argument that Solicitor General Verrilli and Justices Breyer and Kagan made during oral argument: with a substantial number of same-sex couples raising children, including children they adopted, there is an Equal Protection Clause argument for not excluding them from the recognition and rights of marriage.

Chief Justice Roberts's dissent emphasized the distinction between legislators and judges, which agrees with the general argument I am making. His opinion relies heavily on *Lochner* and *Glucksberg*: the former is the negative example and the latter the positive one concerning how to interpret non-enumerated rights, or substantive due process. The *Glucksberg* Court, including Justice Souter's lengthy and careful concurring opinion in addition to Chief Justice Rehnquist's court opinion, presents a moderate approach to substantive due process. In *Obergefell*, Chief Justice Roberts charged the Court with using the non-enumerated right to privacy/autonomy to engage in the kind of judicial policy-making that the *Lochner* Court did with economic rights under the concept of liberty of contract as preventing any state regulation of wages or hours of employment.[71]

Stripped of its shiny rhetorical gloss, the majority's argument is that the Due Process Clause gives same-sex couples a fundamental right to marry because it will be good for them and for society. If I were a legislator, I would certainly consider that view as a matter of social policy. But as a judge, I find the majority's position indefensible as a matter of constitutional law.[72]

While the Chief Justice could not resist deriding Justice Kennedy's emphasis on dignity,[73] he did make the more sober and telling point that Justice Kennedy wants to enshrine John Stuart Mill's "harm principle" in the Constitution.

As Judge Henry Friendly once put it, echoing Justice Holmes's dissent in *Lochner*, the Fourteenth Amendment does not enact John Stuart Mill's *On Liberty* any more than it enacts Herbert Spencer's *Social Statics*.[74]

Chief Justice Roberts's opinion did not address the number of same-sex couples who had children, often through adoption. The Respondents' position, based on their brief and the oral argument, is that the new definition of marriage is likely to have unintended negative consequences. In oral argument, Respondents' attorney focused on the possible negative effect on heterosexual couples. He did not suggest that it's too soon to know what effect being raised by two men or two women will have on children when they become adults, especially if they become—as some will—parents. In addition, a concern about recognition and benefits could have yielded a Vermont style solution, where the Court says that since same-sex couples are legally able to adopt children they should be entitled to the same state benefits, in the form of either civil union or domestic partnership status or marriage.[75] Beyond that, should the state not be able to legislate a preference for traditional marriage while allowing even same-sex couples to adopt children? Must the lesser right (adoption) imply the greater one (marriage)?

Each dissenting justice wrote an opinion. Justice Scalia's brief dissent, which I mentioned, echoed Chief Justice Roberts's.[76]

Justice Thomas began his dissent by calling for a reconsideration of the entire doctrine of substantive due process.[77] A more pertinent part of his opinion concerns his contention that the framers understood constitutional liberty as a freedom from government restraint, not a right to government benefits.

> [I]t would have included a right to engage in the very same activities that petitioners have been left free to engage in—making vows, holding religious ceremonies celebrating those vows, raising children, and otherwise enjoying the society of one's spouse—without government interference.[78]

What Justice Thomas said could be used to distinguish the privacy/autonomy issue in a case like *Lawrence*—in which a state law criminalizes homosexual activity—from the question why a government recognizes marriage as an institution. Of course, on that basis, Justice Thomas should not have joined the majority in striking down the Texas anti-sodomy law. Instead, he called it "uncommonly silly" while voting to uphold it.[79]

Justice Alito's brief dissent quoted substantially from his *Windsor* dissent to suggest that the implied change in the definition of marriage would have a deleterious effect on the institution.[80]

Summary

The Supreme Court decided that the Fourteenth Amendment's Due Process Clause by itself and in conjunction with the Equal Protection Clause required each state to permit same-sex couples to marry on the same terms as opposite-sex couples.[81] The primary ground for this decision was the fundamental right to marry, which the Court extended to same-sex couples for the first time. While Justice Kennedy's court opinion never discussed the level of scrutiny, the implication of such a holding was that strict scrutiny applied. Moreover, the emphasis the Court gave to what it called over- and under-inclusion was consistent with at least a "heightened" scrutiny.

In extending the fundamental right to marry to same-sex couples, the Court redefined marriage as a "two person union," not a

union of a man and a woman. The dissenting justices thought that
the decision should have been left to the political process. From their
perspective, the Court was contradicting its *Washington v. Glucksberg* precedent on the scope of non-enumerated rights: they had to
be "deeply rooted in the Nation's history and tradition."[82] Even Justice Souter's more generous formulation of substantive due process
in his *Glucksberg* concurrence urged caution:

> It is no justification for judicial intervention merely to identify a
> reasonable resolution of contending values that differs from the
> terms of the legislation under review. It is only when the legisla-
> tion's justifying principle, critically valued, is so far from being
> commensurate with the individual interest as to be arbitrarily or
> pointlessly applied that the statute must give way.[83]

Justice Souter's formulation does not apply to the issue in the
same-sex marriage case precisely, since the state's interest is not in
the individual so much as in the parties to the marriage and the an-
ticipated offspring. And the question in *Obergefell* concerns the
constitutional permissibility of retaining the traditional definition
of marriage, despite a changed understanding of the status of homosexuality and, hence, the constitutional rights of homosexuals.[84]
Accepting the correctness of the earlier gay rights decisions, is it
constitutional to protect "gay sex but not gay marriage?"[85] Constitutional scholars generally concluded that the *Lawrence* decision either by itself or in conjunction with the *Windsor* decision implied
the constitutional requirement of an equal right to marry.[86]

If we look at the constitutional issue from the perspective of the
Equal Protection Clause, then the Court might have considered
whether to follow the Justice Department and deem sexual orientation a quasi-suspect classification. But if it did not want to explore
that option, it could have considered its approach in *Romer v. Evans*,
as well as its approach in the sex discrimination cases in the early
1970s. In *Romer*, homosexuals were singled out for exclusion from
every state and local law that protected a series of classes of persons
liable to discrimination. And in *Reed* and *Frontiero*, the Court inval-

idated generalizations about men and women that had the effect of either denying women an opportunity to administer an estate or requiring them to prove the dependency of their spouses for benefits when men did not have to do that.

If "rational basis with bite," to use Gunther's phrase, accounts for the Court's *Reed* and *Frontiero* decisions, as well as *Romer v. Evans*, and if we assume the Court did not have to move to heightened scrutiny for sex classifications, but that outworn stereotypes would not suffice to justify a differential treatment of men and women, what do we make of this same-sex marriage case?

Scholars who advocated same-sex marriage and/or approved of the Court's decision take a broad view of the Equal Protection Clause, with a willingness to take account of public sentiment if it seems that a given decision will meet with strong opposition[87] or they contend that there was no defensible argument in opposition to same-sex marriage.[88] Such a position is similar to the moral philosophic position, identified with John Stuart Mill, that Judge Posner introduced in his circuit court opinion and that Chief Justice Roberts attributed to Justice Kennedy's formulation of the issue in the case.

Keeping in mind that the question before the Court was the constitutionality, not the wisdom, of traditional marriage laws, I do not find these positions in support of *Obergefell* persuasive. Balkin illustrates what he means by "living originalism" in his post-*Obergefell* blog post with this remark: "[W]e should ask what the principles of class legislation, caste legislation, and equality before the law mean in practice in today's world in the context of gays and lesbians who seek the right to marry."[89] Laws tend to classify, and most of the modes of classification have not been understood to violate the Constitution. But this broad reading of the Equal Protection Clause takes away from the legislature and grants to the courts the final authority to say which classifications satisfy the Constitution and which do not.[90]

Judge Posner clearly changed his mind on the constitutionality of same-sex marriage, but he does not acknowledge such in his blistering critique of Respondents' defense of its marriage laws in his Seventh Circuit court opinion. His earlier position reflected the combination of his libertarianism and his pragmatism. In his blogs and a book review, Judge Posner supported in principle an individual contract approach to marriage, but he stopped short of advocating that traditional marriage laws were unconstitutional, because he judged popular support to be lacking for such a ruling. This position resembles the "minimalism" that Cass Sunstein espouses;[91] he too supported same-sex marriage after *Lawrence* but felt there was not yet adequate popular support for such a decision.[92] The implication must be that judging is lawmaking by another name, but for it to work the decisions of nonpolitically responsible judges must proceed in small steps, to prevent a refusal by the public to accept the judicial decision.

In a post-*Obergefell* essay, Marty Lederman presented a different defense of the decision. While he disagreed with Judge Posner for suggesting that "bigotry" accounted for the states' refusal to change their marriage laws to include same-sex couples, he nonetheless wrote that "the principal *real* reason that many states have prohibited same-sex marriage is simply because their legislators and/or their constituents morally disapprove of, or are deeply discomfited by, homosexuality."[93]

That statement may more accurately describe what supporters of same-sex marriage attribute to opponents than it does justice to those who advocate marriage as the union of a man and a woman. As Lederman acknowledged, Justice Alito referred to the concerns about the negative effects that might result from the substitution of "two person union" for the traditional definition. The Supreme Court, and most of the lower courts, sided with the experts who testified and submitted briefs affirming that same-sex couples were as capable of raising children as opposite-sex couples were. This testimony and the reluctance of courts to accept any arrangement, such as civil unions, that differentiated one union from another, were probably decisive. And yet, apart from the suggestion that social science experts may have divided along partisan lines,[94] the time frame for discovering problems makes it very difficult for advocates of tradition. Amy Wax put it this way:

> To satisfy social science standards, conservatives must come forward with data that systematically compares [sic] the effects of established arrangements with innovations they resist. In most cases, this circle cannot be squared. The data either do not yet exist or are radically inconclusive. The requirement to produce rational or scientific justification in the political arena also ensures that remote and collective effects get little weight.[95]

To a majority of the Supreme Court justices, and to almost all of the lower federal court judges, the states resisting same-sex marriage carried the burden of proving that such a change would be harmful. That narrows the range of legislative deliberation and choice.

CHAPTER EIGHT

Conclusion

Reconciling Judicial Review
with Republican Government
under the American Constitution

I HAVE ATTEMPTED TO ILLUSTRATE HOW THE POLITICAL AND LEGAL controversy over same-sex marriage in the United States highlights important features of American constitutionalism. My principal concern has been to present and assess the work of the courts in light of the tension, inherent in the Constitution, between judicial review and republican government. The Founders' commitment to written constitutions, for the states as well as the nation, reflects a judgment that fundamental principles and rules of governance should be set down so that everyone knows the basic rule of law. At the federal level, this included the construction of a separate and independent judiciary. And here is where a tension arises between an independent judiciary and consent of the governed. While I think it was generally understood that the federal courts would review laws "arising under this Constitution,"—even Jefferson thought so in 1789, when he gave it as a reason for supporting a bill of rights—the scope of that judicial review could not possibly be known with any certainty. What, for example, does "contrary to the manifest tenor," the phrase in Federalist 78, tell us about any difficult constitutional case? And as much as it is "the proper and peculiar province of the courts" to interpret the laws, including the Constitution (also from Federalist 78), Federalist 10 reminds us that the line between what could be called "political" rights and "vested" rights, meaning rights set by the legislative process and rights determined by courts, is not always clear. Given the framers' assumption that the courts would follow the common law tradition and work from earlier decisions, either by following them, distinguishing them, or overturning them, it is not surprising that judicial review in practice has threatened to become judicial supremacy, thereby overcoming the self-government part of modern republicanism.

The same-sex marriage controversy in America is a perfect example of this tension between judicial review and republican government. The political question, which was over the wisdom, or desirability, of the proposed change in marriage laws, easily lent itself (as Tocqueville foresaw) to a constitutional controversy, and hence to ultimate resolution by the Supreme Court. In closing, I want first to point to other controversies that have been resolved in the courts and finally in the Supreme Court; some have resulted in judicial decisions favoring conservative opinions about rights; some have resulted in decisions upholding the legislative action. Then I want to turn back to same-sex marriage to indicate what distinguishes that controversy from the others. Finally, I close with some reflections on future controversies arising out of the Court's *Obergefell* decision.

The Supreme Court's major abortion decisions are perhaps most like its gay rights decisions. The continuing controversy over the *Roe* and *Casey* decisions might have been treated more moderately if the Supreme Court had distinguished between the Texas law, which prevented abortion unless the woman's life was at risk, and the Georgia law, which established more extensive categories for abortion and also required the approval of a group of medical professionals. A decision invalidating Texas's law but upholding Georgia's would have provided a space for legislative deliberation and decision while also recognizing the legitimate interests of pregnant women.[1] The equivalent result for gay rights would have been for the Court to follow Vermont's Supreme Court and observe that if a state allows same-sex couples to adopt children, they must provide the same benefits to that family that opposite-sex couples receive when they marry. That would have left it to the state legislatures to opt for a form of civil union or domestic partnership, as it was called in California, or for marriage.[2]

The case that Michigan relied on to support leaving the marriage question to the legislatures was *Schuette v. Coalition to Defend Affirmative Action*, which upheld Michigan's constitutional referendum prohibiting race-conscious affirmative action.[3] So far there are five votes on the Court to support the constitutionality of affirmative action, as long as it is applied on an individualized ("holistic") basis. The Schuette case simply affirmed that the people could decide not to have their state schools use race in admissions.[4] Then, on June 26, 2016, the Supreme Court, on a vote of 5-to-3, upheld the University of Texas at Austin's hybrid affirmative action program. Justice Kennedy wrote the court opinion sustaining the University's reliance on admission of a fixed percentage of students from each public high school in the state, supplemented by a "holistic review" that took account of racial diversity as well as other factors.[5]

Two cases reflecting what could be called "judicial activism" on the right are the Court's First Amendment decisions regarding campaign finance and its Second Amendment decisions on gun control. The Court's decision in *Citizens United v. Federal Election Commission* struck down the Bipartisan Campaign Reform Act of 2002, which had prohibited corporations and unions from spending money on electioneering communications.[6] This decision opened the floodgates of campaign spending from rich individuals and corporate political action committees.[7] Not only does such spending give the impression that the rich control American politics, but the candidates and their campaigns have no control over these funds. The Court's strong free speech decision took the decision away from Congress. Moreover, this started with the Court's decision in *Buckley v. Valeo* (1976), which upheld contribution limits but struck down all expenditure limits. The Court's major contention was that the effort to "equalize" contributions, and hence speech, was against the central purpose of the First Amendment. Of course the law did not truly aim at "equalizing" anything, only at setting some ceilings on campaign expenditures.

As for gun control, in *District of Columbia v. Heller*, the Court concluded that the Second Amendment was not limited to its perambulatory "A well regulated Militia, being necessary to the security of a free State," but rather that "the right of the people to keep and bear Arms, shall not be infringed" guaranteed an individual right to own handguns in Washington, DC.[8] Judge J. Harvie Wilkinson III called this 5-to-4 decision an example of "originalist activism."[9]

In contrast to those two opinions, the Court upheld a very unpopular condemnation proceeding in New London, Connecticut in 2005.[10] Petitioners were two elderly women who were forced to sell their homes because they were in the path of an approved city-wide development plan that was supposed to produce jobs and tax revenue. The plan involved clearing the property so that a pharmaceutical company could put a research facility on site. The Court, in a 5-to-4 opinion by Justice Stevens, upheld the plan, citing precedent for the proposition that the "public use" for the sake of which private property could be taken did not have to involve publically owned property. The conservative justices dissented and some members of Congress were livid over the decision.[11] This is a good example, however, of a judicial decision upholding as constitutional action that was not necessarily good public policy. The local government decided to support the redevelopment and to allow the public power of condemnation to apply to all property in the projected development. That did not prevent partisan criticism of the decision from charging the Court with judicial activism.[12]

As Justice Stevens pointed out in a lecture he gave on the case the following fall, all that was needed to prevent such action was either state legislation or local regulation.[13]

The two recent decisions on the Affordable Care Act[14] also illustrate the difference between constitutionality and wisdom. I think that reflects the perspective of Chief Justice Roberts, who voted to uphold the ACA when it was originally challenged, albeit on tax and spend grounds only, not on commerce clause grounds, and then wrote the court opinion in the 6-to-3 decision to interpret the law to allow federal subsidies for individuals who purchased their health insurance policies from federal exchanges as well as state exchanges.[15]

There is something distinctive about the Court's treatment of the same-sex marriage controversy. My earlier discussion of how commentators and Judge Posner dismissed Respondents' arguments in support of their traditional marriage laws reflects more than a commitment to a broad view of equality. It also reflects an inappropriate conflation of motive and purpose; that religious convictions motivated many who opposed same-sex marriage should not taint the purposes served by the traditional understanding of marriage.

The case for the traditional notion of marriage as the union of a man and a woman has a natural support that does not depend upon Biblical revelation. And that natural support also distinguishes the limiting of marriage to a heterosexual union from a ban on interracial marriage. Our gender-neutral view of law should not blind us to the natural differences between the sexes. The position that children are best reared by a father and a mother (and by their biological parents in the best case) is not refuted by equal work opportunities for women. And while religious belief supports the related preference for procreation over artificial forms of reproduction, the natural principle of love of one's own also does. Conservative supporters of gay marriage such as Andrew Sullivan and Jonathan Rauch both acknowledged the natural limitations of homosexuality precisely on that point.

In chapter three I examined the case for and the case against same-sex marriage and concluded that the clear benefits for some outweigh the speculative harms for others. In addition, as long as same-sex couples were going to live together and have children, it made sense to allow the couples to marry. But I do not think that the Constitution should have been interpreted to require that resolution to the controversy.

Given the widespread acceptance today of homosexuality as a natural manifestation of human sexuality, I do not anticipate substantial resistance to the *Obergefell* decision.[16] And the Supreme

Court is likely to be more tolerant of religious belief in the context of free exercise claims against having to recognize same-sex marriages in all commercial contexts than it was receptive to arguments from tradition in support of marriage as the union of a man and a woman. In light of the Religious Freedom Restoration Act (RFRA),[17] the Court will surely protect free exercise claims, as it has already done.[18] That could mean, for example, that universities which receive federal money but which object to same-sex marriage may not be required to accommodate same-sex married couples in married student housing.[19] The controversy will be more difficult in states with civil rights laws that prohibit discrimination on the basis of sexual orientation.[20]

I do think that *Obergefell* is the kind of decision that will reinforce the partisanship which has emerged over the appointment and confirmation process for federal judges, including the lower court judges as well as the Supreme Court Justices. We have seen this recently, with the Republican-controlled Senate refusing to call hearings, let alone to have a vote, on President Obama's nomination of Merrick Garland to the Supreme Court after the death of Justice Scalia—followed by the Republican-controlled Senate's suspension of the sixty-vote filibuster rule for Supreme Court nominees in order to confirm Judge Neil Gorsuch, President Trump's choice for the Court, because 44 of the 48 Democratic Senators refused to permit an up-or-down vote.[21] We will have further occasion to ponder the importance of distinguishing between constitutionality and wisdom for the sake of maintaining our respect for the importance of the democratic political process and the courts.

Notes

Chapter One

1. 135 S. Ct. 2584 (2015).
2. Id. at 2593. See also Justice Kennedy's opinion *Lawrence v. Texas*, 539 U.S. 558, 562 (2003):

> Liberty protects the person from unwarranted government intrusions into a dwelling or other private places. In our tradition the State is not omnipresent in the home. And there are other spheres of our lives and existence, outside the home, where the State should not be a dominant presence. Freedom extends beyond spatial bounds. Liberty presumes an autonomy of self that includes freedom of thought, belief, expression, and certain intimate conduct. The instant case involves liberty of the person both in its spatial and more transcendent dimensions.

Compare that with his part of the joint opinion in *Planned Parenthood of Southeastern Pa. v. Casey*, 505 U.S. 833 (1992) at 851 ("At the heart of liberty is the right to define one's own concept of existence, of meaning, of the universe, and of the mystery of human life. Beliefs about these matters could not define the attributes of personhood were they formed under compulsion of the State").

3. *Obergefell* at 2598.
4. *Baker v. Nelson*, 409 U.S. 810 (1972).
5. *Obergefell* at 2599.
6. Id. at 2599–2601.
7. Id. at 2602.
8. Id. at 2611.
9. Philip Kurland, "The True Wisdom of the Bill of Rights," in *The Bill of Rights and the Modern State*, eds. Geoffrey Stone, Richard A. Epstein, and Cass R. Sunstein (Univ. of Chicago Press, 1992), 7–8.
10. The highest courts in the several states also exercise a similar scrutiny, and if they interpret state constitutions to restrict legislatures more

extensively than the Federal Constitution does, those decisions are final. I discuss the significance of this practice below.

11. State courts have interpreted their respective state constitutions in these cases, not the federal Constitution. However, as I show in the chapters on the major state high court decisions, those constitutional arguments draw heavily on federal constitutional law precedents. The state courts assert that their decisions are based on their own state constitutions in order to insulate their decisions from review, and possible reversal, by the U.S. Supreme Court.

12. *McCulloch v. Maryland*, 17 U.S. 316, 407 (1819).

13. I discuss Publius' argument for judicial review in chapter two.

14. I discuss this more fully in subsequent chapters.

15. See *Walz v. Tax Commission of the City of New York*, 397 U.S. 664, 669 (1970) and *Locke v. Davey*, 540 U.S. 712, 718–719 (2004).

16. I discuss the Court's development of different levels of scrutiny in chapter four.

17. The Supreme Court upheld Minnesota's marriage law, which did not allow same-sex marriage, in *Baker v. Nelson*, 409 U.S. 810 (1972), but no serious litigation effort was made until two decades later.

18. *Baehr v. Lewin*, 852 P.2d 44 (Haw. 1993). I discuss this case in chapter five. Strict scrutiny puts the burden of proof on the government. I discuss the various levels of scrutiny the Supreme Court and state courts employ below.

19. I discuss DOMA, including the Supreme Court's decision to invalidate section 3, in chapter six.

20. *Dean v. District of Columbia*, 653 A. 2d 307 (D.C. App. 1995). For citations to the state court decisions, see chapter five.

21. Wikipedia, Same-Sex Marriage in the United States (accessed 7/9/2015). The dates refer to when the law was enacted. In Maine, voters approved a referendum, but the constitution refers to this as the "People's Legislative power." I am citing Wikipedia because I have not found a more complete source for this information on same-sex marriage in the United States.

22. *New York Times*, December 18, 2010.

23. *Perry v. Schwarzenegger*, 704 F. Supp. 2d 921, 929 (N.D. Cal. 2010).

24. *Perry v. Brown*, 671 F.3d 1052 (9th Cir. 2012).

25. *Hollingsworth v. Perry*, 133 S. Ct. 2652 (2013). I discuss the Proposition 8 case in chapter six.

26. 133 S. Ct. 2675 (2013). I discuss this case in chapter six.

27. *Garden State Equality v. Paula Dow*, L-1729-11. Governor Chris Christie sought a stay so he could appeal, but the state Supreme Court denied it, implying that the decision would be upheld. The governor then dropped the appeal.

28. *Griego and Keil v. Oliver*, New Mexico Supreme Court, December 19, 2013.

29. Lambda Legal, "Favorable Rulings in Marriage Equality Cases Since *U.S. v. Windsor*, as of June 24, 2015," www.lambdalegal.org/sites/default/files/post-windsor_cases_ruling_in_favor_of_marriage_equality_claims_as_of_6.24.2015.pdf (emphases omitted). Note 1 to the material I quote states: "Only one federal appellate ruling, three federal trial court rulings, and one state trial court ruling have parted ways with this virtual unanimity since *Windsor.*"

30. Alexis de Tocqueville, *Democracy in America*, ed. and trans. Harvey Mansfield and Delba Winthrop (Univ. of Chicago Press, 2000), 280.

31. In his book *Same-Sex Marriage in the United States: The Road to the Supreme Court* (Rowman and Littlefield, 2013), Jason Pierceson, after identifying Alexander Bickel and Ronald Dworkin with the different "normative" positions on judicial review, describes his own position as examining "to what extent courts create change in society through the process of litigation" (4). His assessment does not discuss judicial review in relation to republican government. In both his conclusion and his epilogue, written for the 2014 paperback edition after the *Windsor* case, Pierceson emphasized social change. That seems to mean court-assisted progressive change, with enough popular support to sustain it. See 239–41 and 254–55.

32. *Michigan v. Long*, 463 U.S, 1032, 1035 (1983) stated that the Supreme Court would not review the highest decision of a state court if that decision was based on an "adequate and independent state ground."

33. I use this term because the highest court in both New York and Maryland is called the Court of Appeals.

Chapter Two

1. Consider *Roe v. Wade*, 410 U.S. 113 (1973) and *Planned Parenthood v. Casey*, 505 U.S. 833 (1992), on abortion, and *Bush v. Gore*, 531 U.S. 98 (2000), on the contested presidential election of 2000.

2. In his discussion of the subject, J. Harvie Wilkinson III identifies Justice Black and Judge Robert Bork as advocates of "originalism" and Justice Brennan as an advocate of the "living constitution." See Wilkinson,

Cosmic Constitutional Theory: Why Americans Are Losing Their Inalienable Right to Self-Governance (Oxford Univ. Press, 2012), 33–45.

3. Professor Karl Coplan, of Pace Law School, made that observation at a panel discussion on judging at Middlebury College in the fall of 2010. He is a former student of mine. I think his statement is true of most constitutional scholars, based on the ones I have studied.

4. See Judge J. Harvie Wilkinson III's account of "value judgments" in *Cosmic Constitutional Theory*, 62, 69, 74, 77.

5. Gerald Gunther, "Foreword: In Search of Evolving Doctrine on a Changing Court: A Model for a Newer Equal Protection," 86 *Harv. L. Rev.* 1 (Nov. 1972). I discuss this position in chapter four in connection with the Court's development of a special level of scrutiny for sex discrimination cases.

6. Tocqueville, *Democracy in America*, 257.

7. 5 U.S. 137 (1803).

8. See Thomas Jefferson's letters to James Madison from Paris (March 15, 1789) and to Spencer Roane from Poplar Forest (September 6, 1789) in *The Portable Jefferson*, ed. Merrill D. Peterson (Penguin, 1977), 438–40, 561–64.

9. 12 S & R Penn. Rep. 330 Pa. (1825).

10. See his plurality opinion in *Colegrove v. Green*, 328 U.S. 549 (1946).

11. *Baker v. Carr*, 369 U.S. 186 (1962).

12. *Nixon v. United States*, 506 U.S. 224 (1993). While the case involved the form of the trial, it probably is good precedent for the meaning of an impeachable offense, including "high crimes and misdemeanors."

13. 60 U.S. 393.

14. See Lincoln's Springfield Speech delivered June 26, 1857 in *Abraham Lincoln: His Speeches and Writings*, ed. Roy P. Basler (The World Publishing Co., 1946), 352, 355.

15. Lincoln made this point in his First Inaugural Address, March 4, 1861. See id. at 579, 585.

16. James MacGregor Burns, *Packing the Court: The Rise of Judicial Power and the Coming Crisis of the Supreme Court* (Penguin, 2009), 2 (italics in original).

17. Id.

18. "The president would announce flatly that he or she would not accept the Supreme Court's verdicts because the power of judicial emasculation of legislation was not—and never had been—in the Constitution. The president would invite the partisans of judicial supremacy to try to write that authority into the Constitution by proposing a constitutional amend-

ment. Through their representatives in Congress and the state legislatures, the American people would be given the choice denied them in 1803: to establish in the Constitution the power of judicial supremacy, or to reject that power. Only by this route could judicial rule be legitimated, that is, 'constitutionalized.'" Id. at 253.

19. Id. at 259.

20. Larry D. Kramer, *The People Themselves: Popular Constitutionalism and Judicial Review* (Oxford Univ. Press, 2004), 7.

21. Id. at 24–27.

22. He cites Gordon Wood for likening such action to the state interposition that Jefferson and Madison advocated in their Kentucky and Virginia Resolutions, or to the Massachusetts colonists' resistance to the Stamp Act. Id. at 63.

23. See Essays of Brutus, number XI, in *The Anti-Federalist*, ed. Herbert J. Storing (Univ. of Chicago Press, 1985), an abridgment of Storing's *The Complete Writings of the Anti-Federalist* (Univ. of Chicago Press, 1981). The Essays of Brutus are presented in their entirety in the abridgment; they are in volume II of the complete edition.

24. Federalist 78, in Robert Scigliano, ed., *The Federalist* (Modern Library, 2001), 498.

25. Locke, *Two Treatises of Government*, ed. Peter Laslett (Cambridge Univ. Press, 1960). See chap. 13, sec. 149, p. 367 for Locke's statement that "this Power of the People can never take place till the Government be dissolved," and chap. 19 for his discussion of dissolution.

26. See Kramer's discussion of this issue in *The People Themselves* (45), and Federalist 49.

27. See Madison on the difference between ancient and modern representation in Federalist 63 (Scigliano, 406–7).

28. Kramer, *The People Themselves*, 76; this is quoted from James Madison, *Notes of Debates in the Federal Convention of 1787*, ed. Adrienne Koch (Norton, 1987), 336–37.

29. Madison, *Notes of Debates*, 338.

30. For the view that the Supreme Court is sensitive to public opinion, see Barry Friedman, *The Will of the People: How Public Opinion Has Influenced the Supreme Court and Shaped the Meaning of the Constitution* (FSG, 2009).

31. Kramer, *The People Themselves*, 77.

32. Federalist 78 (Scigliano, 497). Hamilton referred expressly to the prohibitions on bills of attainder and ex post facto laws in article I, section 9.

33. See Brutus XI, in Storing, *The Anti-Federalist*, especially 163–65.

34. Kramer, *The People Themselves*, 146. This quote comes from a letter that Madison wrote to an unnamed recipient in 1834. Kramer's source is *4 Letters and Other Writings of James Madison* (1884), 349–50. Another source dates the letter December 1834. See http://rotunda.upress.virginia.edu/founders/default.xqy?keys=FOEA-print-02-02-02-3067.

35. Id. at 146–47.

36. Federalist 63 (Scigliano, 405–7).

37. *Cooper v. Aaron*, 358 U.S. 1 (1958).

38. *United States v. Morrison*, 529 U.S. 598 (2000), quoted by Kramer at 225–26.

39. Kramer, *The People Themselves*, 208.

40. See id. at 249 for Kramer's list.

41. Id. at 253.

42. Federalist 63 (Scigliano, 407).

43. See Wilkinson's discussion of this in his *Cosmic Constitutional Theory*, chapter two.

44. See Justice Scalia's dissent in *Planned Parenthood v. Casey*, 505 U.S. 833 (1992). In contrast, Chief Justice Marshall decided *Fletcher v. Peck* partly on the basis of the contract clause and partly on the basis of "principles of natural justice." See 10 U.S. 87 (1810).

45. See *Michael H. v. Gerald D.*, 491 U.S. 110 (1989), where Justice Scalia's attempt to introduce such a position in a footnote caused Justice O'Connor, who otherwise joined in Scalia's opinion to take issue with him. See Justice Scalia's footnote 6 at 127 and Justice O'Connor's partial concurrence at 132.

46. See Antonin Scalia, *A Matter of Interpretation* (Princeton Univ. Press, 1997), 138–39, responding to Laurence Tribe's comment about Scalia's vote in the flag burning cases. As for *Brown v. Board of Education*, Justice Scalia had argued in a 1990 dissent that the Thirteenth and Fourteenth Amendments, understood in light of a persistent constitutional challenge to "separate but equal" supported Justice Harlan's dissent in *Plessy v. Ferguson*. The opinion is Justice Scalia's dissent in *Rutan v. Republican Party*, 497 U.S. 62, 95–96, note 1; it was quoted in Ronald Turner, "A Critique of Justice Antonin Scalia's Originalist Defense of *Brown v. Board of Education*," 62 *UCLA L. Rev. Disc.* 170. Robert Bork provided a similar argument about Brown in *The Tempting of America: The Political Seduction of the Law* (The Free Press, 1990), 81–82.

47. The relevant cases are *Furman v. Georgia*, 408 U.S. 238 (1972), and *Gregg v. Georgia*, 428 U.S. 153 (1976). Wilkinson discusses this in *Cosmic Constitutional Theory*, 25–26.

48. Jack Balkin, *Living Originalism* (Harvard Univ. Press, 2011), 4.

49. Id. at 7.

50. Id. at 10.

51. He cites the women's movement of the 1960s and 1970s in the first chapter and *Brown v. Board of Education* and *Roe v. Wade* in a concluding chapter.

52. Id. at 17.

53. Id. at 230 ff.

54. Id. at 270. After *Obergefell*, Balkin wrote a blog post expressing support for the Court's decision. See "Living Originalism and Same-Sex Marriage," on Balkinization, April 7, 2015.

55. Balkin, *Living Originalism*, 286. Alexander Bickel refers to the conflict between judicial review and the principle of consent of the governed as the "counter-majoritarian difficulty." See *The Least Dangerous Branch: The Supreme Court at the Bar of Politics* (Bobbs Merrill, 1962), 16–17.

56. Balkin, *Living Originalism*, 287.

57. Id. at 296.

58. Richard Posner, *Law, Pragmatism, and Democracy* (Harvard Univ. Press, 2003), 233.

59. U.S. Const. art. I, § 18.

60. Id. art. VI, clause 2: "This Constitution, and the Laws of the United States which shall be made in pursuance thereof; and all Treaties, made, or which shall be made, under the Law of the Land; and the Judges in every State shall be bound thereby, any Thing in the Constitution or Laws of any State to the Contrary notwithstanding."

61. See *Cooper v. Aaron*, 358 U.S. 1 (1958). The Tea Party movement may constitute a new challenge to federal supremacy; it surely favors a limited federal government.

62. *Michigan v. Long*, 463 U.S. 1032, 1035 (1983).

63. "State Constitutions and the Protection of Individual Rights," 90 *Harv. L. Rev.* 489 (Jan. 1977).

64. Kenji Yoshino discusses the conflict between the different groups supporting same-sex marriage in his recent book, *Speak Now: Marriage Equality on Trial; The Story of* Hollingsworth v. Perry (Crown, 2015), 43–50.

65. Hawaii's Supreme Court interpreted its state constitution to require strict scrutiny for classification by sex. I discuss the U.S. Supreme Court's treatment of levels of scrutiny in chapter four.

66. The Full Faith and Credit Clause reads: "Full Faith and Credit shall be given in each State to the public Acts, Records, and judicial Proceedings of every other States. And the Congress may by general Laws prescribe the

Manner in which such Acts, Records and Proceedings shall be proved, and the Effect thereof" (art. IV, § 1).

67. Pub. L. 104-199, § 2(a), 110 Stat. 2419 (1996) (codified at 28 U.S.C. § 1738C (2012)).

68. See Larry Kramer, "Same-Sex Marriage, Conflict of Laws, and the Unconstitutional Public Policy Exception," 106 *Yale L.J.* 1965 (1997); presumably Cass Sunstein had something like this in mind also, though he might have also allowed the state to employ the strong public policy objection. See the excerpt from his testimony in *Same-Sex Marriage: Pro and Con*, 214–15.

69. "The first sentence did not command that any particular effect by given to the statute, record, or judgment; nor did it contain conflict of laws or jurisdictional commands to the states concerning the statutes, records or judgments of other states. The evidence also indicates that the significant power being granted to the national government in the clause was granted in the second sentence to Congress in the form of the power to declare the effects that state statutes, records, and judgments had to be given in other states." Ralph U. Whitten, "Full Faith and Credit for Dummies," 38 *Creighton L. Rev.* 465, 466 (2005).

70. The status of the Full Faith and Credit Clause as it applied to same-sex marriage was mooted by the Supreme Court's decision in *Obergefell*. Likewise, section 2 of DOMA, which affirmed the "strong public policy exception" as applied to marriage laws, was effectively invalidated.

71. *Baehr v. Miike*, 1999 Haw. LEXIS 391, December 9, 1999, for the Summary Disposition Order.

72. CNN Politics 4 November 2009 "Maine Rejects Same-Sex Marriage Law." The vote was 53 percent to 47 percent.

73. I discuss the California case, which led to the challenge in federal court, in chapter five.

74. The alternative would be for two-thirds of the state legislatures to direct Congress to call a constitutional convention. See article V of the Constitution.

Chapter Three

1. Justice Felix Frankfurter is known for making this distinction. See his dissent in *West Virginia State Board of Education v. Barnette*, 319 U.S. 642 (1943), in which he cites the work of James Bradley Thayer, "The Origin and Scope of the American Doctrine of Constitutional Law," 7 *Harv. L.*

Rev. 129 (Oct. 1893). Long before Thayer, however, James Wilson made the point in the Federal Convention. See the text accompanying n. 28, chapter two.

2. "The nature of injustice is that we may not always see it in our own times. . . . When new insight reveals discord between the Constitution's central protections and a received legal stricture [the limitation of marriage to the union of a man and a woman], a claim to liberty must be addressed." *Obergefell*, 135 S. Ct. at 2598; see the text quoted at n. 7, chapter one.

3. Respondents' brief before the Supreme Court in the Proposition 8 case, *Hollingsworth v. Perry*, 133 S. Ct. 2652 (2013), started with the importance of marriage and then turned to equality. See Introduction, p. 1, of the brief for Perry et al. at www.scotusblog.com.

4. George Chauncey identifies three factors: a growth in the visibility and acceptance of lesbians and gay men, the devastation of the AIDs virus and the increase in lesbian couples having and/or raising children together. See *Why Marriage? The History Shaping Today's Debate Over Gay Equality* (Basic Books, 2005), chap. 4, especially 95–105.

5. Pub. L. 104-199, § 2(a), 110 Stat. 2419 (1996) (codified at 28 U.S.C. § 1738C (2012)).

6. In the second Creation story, God created Adam and then declared, "It is not good that the man should be alone; I will make him a helpmeet for him" and then created Eve by taking a rib from Adam. "And Adam said, This is now my flesh: she shall be called Woman, because was taken out of Man. Therefore shall a man leave his father and mother and, and, shall cleave unto his wife: and they shall be one flesh." Gen. 2:18, 23, 24 (KJV). A similar statement, without any direct reference to God's taking a rib from Adam to create Eve, appears in Matthew, concluding: "Wherefore they are no more twain, but one flesh. What therefore God hath joined together, let not man put asunder" (Matt. 19:6). In addition, both the Old and the New Testaments contain passages condemning homosexual activity. Lev. 20, 13; Rom. I, 26–27; 1 Cor. 6, 9. Based largely on these Scriptural sources, the 2003 Vatican statement, entitled "Considerations Regarding Proposal to Give Legal Recognition to Unions Between Homosexual Persons," took the position that "marriage exists solely between a man and a woman," and that homosexual acts are "a serious depravity," "intrinsically disordered," and "sins gravely contrary to chastity" (http://www.vatican.va/roman_curia/congregations/cfaith/documents/rc_con_cfaith_doc_20030731_homosexual-unions_en.html).

7. Stephen Macedo devotes chapter 2 of his recent book *Just Married: Same-Sex Couples, Monogamy & the Future of Marriage* (Princeton Univ.

Press, 2015) to this group of scholars. In addition to Finnis and George, it includes Germain Grisez, Patrick Lee, Ryan T. Anderson, and Sherif Girgis, among others.

8. *Summa Theologica*, Question 94, article two, Introduction to pp. 637–38.

9. John Finnis, *Natural Law and Natural Rights*, Clarendon Law Series (Oxford Univ. Press, 1980), 33–34.

10. Id. at 36. "From end to end of his ethical discourses, the primary categories for Aquinas are the 'good' and the 'reasonable'; the 'natural' is, from the point of view of his ethics, a speculative appendage added by way of metaphysical reflection, not a counter with which to advance either to or from the practical prima principia per se nota [first principles, known by themselves]."

11. Id. at 36–37, quoting from Hume's *Treatise on Human Nature*, bk. III, pt. I, sec. 2.

12. Id. at 47.

13. Id.

14. See id. and Hume's note on natural law and teleology (52). Finnis separates Aquinas' ethics from his theology in order to affirm that his natural law teaching does not rely on knowledge of God, or "D," as Finnis symbolizes what he calls "creative uncaused causality" (402). After noting that Plato (and he could have said Aristotle as well) "has no concept of divine law," i.e., revelation, Finnis rejects Plato's and Aristotle's accounts of contemplation as the best life, because of "the deep uncertainty in their knowledge of God's nature and relation to this world and its goods" (397; see also 398). He proceeds to describe Aquinas' natural law, which he acknowledges Aquinas subsumes under Eternal Law, which also comprehends divine law, as "no more than a straightforward application of his general theory of the cause and operation of human understanding in any field of inquiry" (399). And again: "So, for Aquinas, there is nothing extraordinary about man's grasp of the natural law; it is simply one application of man's ordinary power of understanding" (400). By separating Aquinas' theology from his ethics, Finnis wants to affirm the existence of rational ends without giving an account of what makes them possible. But a self-evident truth needs a grounding to connect the predicate with the subject. Finnis interprets Aquinas as expressing himself "metaphorically" when he describes the natural law as man's participation in the eternal law (402). For Finnis, whether that is true or not is beyond our capacity as human beings to know, but such knowledge is apparently not necessary for "human flourishing" and "the basic values grasped by human understanding" (403).

15. James Stoner, "Natural Law, Common Law, and the Constitution," in *Common Law Theory*, ed. Douglas E. Edlin (Cambridge Univ. Press, 2007), 183.

16. Stoner pointed this out at id.

17. John Finnis, "Law, Morality, and 'Sexual Orientation,' " in *Same Sex: Debating the Ethics, Science, and Culture of Homosexuality*, ed. John Corvino (Rowman and Littlefield, 1997), 34–35.

18. Stephen Macedo makes a similar observation in *Just Married*, 44–45, 54ff.

19. Robert P. George and Gerald V. Bradley, "Marriage and the Liberal Imagination," 84 *Geo. L. J.* 301, 304 (Dec. 1995).

20. Sherif Girgis, Ryan T. Anderson, and Robert P. George, *What Is Marriage?: Man and Woman: A Defense* (Encounter Books, 2012), 74.

21. "But one's sex act with one's spouse will not be truly marital—and will not authentically actualize, and allow one in a non-illusory way to experience, one's marriage—if one engages in it while one would be willing in some circumstance(s) to engage in a sex act of a non-marital kind—e.g., adultery, fornication, intentionally sterilized intercourse, solitary masturbation or mutual masturbation (e.g., sodomy) and so forth." Finnis, "Law, Morality," 38. See also Girgis, Anderson, and George at 27–28. Finnis cites a passage in Plato's *Gorgias* in support of his position that "sexual acts cannot in reality be self-giving unless they are acts by which a man and a woman actualize and experience sexually the real giving of themselves to each other in biological, affective, and volitional union in mutual commitment, both open-ended and exclusive . . ." (35). But since Plato's Socrates was arguing against the reduction of the good to the pleasant, especially with the pleasant understood as related to the body, Finnis's interpretation goes a step further than Plato's Socrates in morally disapproving of any activity that is chosen for the sake of pleasure. I do not think that either Plato or Aristotle's treatment of the virtue of moderation is nearly as severe on pleasure as Finnis and his fellow "new natural lawyers" are.

22. See Susan Shell, "The Liberal Case Against Gay Marriage," *The Public Interest* 156 (Summer 2004): 3–16.

23. Finnis, "Law, Morality," 41.

24. Id.

25. Id. at 42.

26. Id. Stephen Macedo, whom Finnis named in this context, replied with an express affirmation of support for moderation.

27. See Richard Posner, *Sex and Reason* (Harvard Univ. Press, 1992), chaps. 4 and 11; and Dean Hamer and Peter Copeland, *The Science of*

Desire: The Search for the Gay Gene and the Biology of Behavior (Simon and Schuster, 1994). For a more recent account—from a biologist—confirming what legal scholar Posner wrote, see Simon LeVay, *Gay, Straight, and the Reason Why: The Science of Sexual Orientation* (Oxford Univ. Press, 2011), chaps. 1 and 11 (conclusions).

28. John Rawls, *A Theory of Justice* (Harvard Univ. Press, 1971).

29. Id. at 14–15.

30. Id. at 15.

31. John Rawls, *Political Liberalism* (Columbia Univ. Press, 2005), 10–11.

32. Id. at 450.

33. Id. at 456.

34. Id. at 443.

35. This was written in 1997, as part of a law review article, or in 1998, as his last revision. See id. at 437, 438.

36. Id. at 456–57.

37. Id. at 457.

38. Id. at 467, n. 60. Rawls treats the abortion controversy in a similarly abrupt manner (243). He later revises his apparent support for a woman's right to abort in the first trimester, but he still gives the impression that any legitimate argument from public reason supports the right (479). In another place, Rawls calls abortion a disputed question and in such a case each side should abide by the outcome of a vote, even if it goes against the Catholic position rejecting abortion. For, Rawls, opponents "need not exercise abortion in their own case" (liv–lv). It is strange that Rawls addresses a vote for abortion; the Supreme Court made the key vote on that issue. Rawls fails to say whether a vote against abortion, say with exceptions for a mother's health, incest, rape, etc., would pass muster with public reason.

39. James Q. Wilson, *The Marriage Problem: How Our Culture Has Weakened Families* (HarperCollins, 2002), 24.

40. Id. at 40–41.

41. "In all or nearly all human societies, marriage is socially approved sexual intercourse between a woman and a man, conceived both as a personal relationship and as an institution, primarily such that any children resulting from the union are—and are understood by the society to be—emotionally, morally, practically, and legally affiliated with both of the parents." David Blankenhorn, *The Future of Marriage* (Encounter Books, 2007), 91.

42. Jonathan Rauch, *Gay Marriage: Why It Is Good for Gays, Good for Straights, and Good for America* (Henry Holt, 2004), 22. See also Andrew Sullivan, *Virtually Normal: An Argument About Homosexuality* (Vintage

Books, 1996), 179–80; Stephen Macedo, "Homosexuality and the Conservative Mind," in 84 *Geo. L.J.* 261 (Dec. 1995); Robin West, *Marriage, Sexuality, and Gender* (Paradigm Publishers, 2007). Macedo also discusses caregiving within and outside of marriage in his recent book, *Just Married*, 106, 133 passim. I return to this point in chapter six.

43. Shell, "Liberal Case Against Gay Marriage," 11.

44. Amy Wax, "The Conservative's Dilemma: Traditional Institutions, Social Change, and Same-Sex Marriage," 42 *San Diego L. Rev.* 1059 (2005).

45. West, *Marriage, Sexuality, and Gender*, 6–7. She notes that the Massachusetts Supreme Court had redefined marriage when it held that that state's constitution prohibited the traditional limitation of marriage to the union of a man and a woman.

46. And at least one, Judith Stacey, whom Blankenhorn highlights as a negative model, supports gay marriage as a way of undermining traditional marriage in order to "promote a democratic, pluralistic expansion of the meaning, practice and politics of family life in the United States. This could help to supplant the destructive sanctity of *the family* with respect for diverse and vibrant *families*." Stacey, *In the Name of the Family*, as quoted in Blankenhorn, *Future of Marriage*, 286–87.

47. E. J. Graff, "Retying the Knot," from the *Nation*, June 24, 1996, quoted in Andrew Sullivan, ed., *Same-Sex Marriage: Pro and Con: A Reader* (Vintage Books, 1997), 135, 137.

48. Evan Wolfson, "Crossing the Threshold: Equal Marriage Rights for Lesbians and Gay Men and the Intra-Community Critique," 21 *N.Y.U. Rev. L. & Soc. Change* 567 (1994–95), quoted in Sullivan, *Same-Sex Marriage*, 144.

49. Sullivan, *Virtually Normal*, 179–80.

50. Id. at 196. For a similar if less poetic statement of the same point, see Rauch, *Gay Marriage*, 100. For a related point, about the importance of the complementarity of male and female, see Dennis O'Brien, "A More Perfect Union," in *Same-Sex Marriage: The Moral and Legal Debate*, 2nd edition, eds. Robert M. Baird and Stuart E. Rosenbaum (Prometheus Books, 2004), 203.

51. Sullivan, *Virtually Normal*, 197–98.

52. Id. at 202.

53. Id. at 203–4.

54. Elizabeth Kristol, "The Marrying Kind," a review of Sullivan's *Virtually Normal*, from Baird and Rosenbaum, *Same-Sex Marriage*, 213; originally published in *First Things* 59 (January 1996).

55. Id. at 214–215.

56. James Q. Wilson, "Against Homosexual Marriage," in Sullivan, *Same-Sex Marriage: Pro and Con*, 2nd edition (Vintage, 2004), 167; Wilson's review was originally published in *Commentary Magazine*, March 1996.

57. Today some researchers claim there is adequate evidence that gay parents are just as able as heterosexual parents. Others claim that the data are not sufficient and that it will take several generations to know the result.

58. Sullivan, *Same-Sex Marriage* (2004), 169.

59. Blankenhorn, *Future of Marriage*, 91.

60. Id. at 133. Blankenhorn's interjection, "that's the whole point," refers to the position of Judith Stacey, who advocated same-sex marriage as a way of undermining marriage as an institution. Blankenhorn agreed with Stacey about the effect of separating procreation from marriage.

61. He refers to divorce, unwed childbearing, and non-marital co-habitation. Id. at 140–41.

62. Id. at 151. The Massachusetts supreme judicial court's opinion, which I discuss in chapter 5, begins: "Marriage is a vital social institution. The exclusive commitment of two individuals to each other nurtures love and mutual support; it brings stability to our society." *Goodridge v. Dept. of Public Health*, 798 N.E.2d 941 (2003).

63. Blankenhorn, *Future of Marriage*, 207 (point 13).

64. Id. at 175.

65. Id. at 181.

66. Id. at 184.

67. See the sources cited at n. 27, chapter three.

68. David Blankenhorn, "How My View on Gay Marriage Changed," *New York Times*, June 22, 2012. Blankenhorn's decision to support marriage among gays and straights surely did not surprise his friend Jonathan Rauch, who wrote the following in his preface to the paperback edition of *The Future of Marriage*:

> The finest achievement of *The Future of Marriage*, in the opinion of this gay writer, is the model it provides of how to discuss gay marriage without animosity toward gay people, and without disrespect for their lives and unions. Blankenhorn has publicly affirmed what he calls 'the equal dignity of homosexual love.' As of this writing, I know of no other gay-marriage opponent who has said those words. . . . In the vexed, polarized context of the gay-marriage debate, there can be no higher compliment than to say that Blankenhorn has written a book about *marriage*.

Chapter Four

1. Vermont District Court Judge Frank Mahady, after lecturing at Middlebury College, in 1985, described the Supremacy Clause as "a single-edged sword." He meant that, while state courts were free under the "adequate and independent state ground[s]" doctrine (see *Michigan v. Long*, 463 U.S. 1032, 1040–41) to interpret their constitutions to protect rights *more extensively* than what the Supreme Court has held the federal Constitution protects, they cannot interpret their constitutions to *restrict* those federally protected rights in any way.

2. 409 U.S. 810 (1972).

3. *Baker v. Nelson*, 191 N.W. 2d 185, 186 (Minn. 1971).

4. Id. at 186–87.

5. 517 U.S. 620.

6. 539 U.S. 558.

7. *McCulloch v. Maryland*, 17 U.S. 316, 421 (1819).

8. I use the term "nominal" to indicate that the Supreme Court's substantive due process decisions in the "Lochner era" could be described as applying strict scrutiny to laws attempting to regulate hours or employment or wages. See *Lochner v. New York*, 198 U.S. 45 (1905).

9. The most important Supreme Court decisions in what is known as the "constitutional revolution of 1937" are *West Coast v. Parrish*, 300 U.S. 379 (1937), and *NLRB v. Jones & Laughlin Steel Corp.*, 301 U.S. 1 (1937).

10. *United States v. Carolene Products Co.*, 304 U.S. 144, 152 n. 4 (1938).

11. 323 U.S. 214 (1944). Justice Black wrote the court opinion upholding, as a wartime emergency measure, the executive order excluding Japanese Americans from their homes indefinitely.

12. *Bolling v. Sharpe*, 347 U.S. 497, 499 (1954). The language led to a formal recognition of strict scrutiny in race cases, and thus the various decisions on affirmative action.

13. 163 U.S. 537 (1896).

14. Id. at 559.

15. *Adarand Constructors, Inc. v. Pena*, 515 U.S. 200, 227 (1995). The Court reiterated this test in its 2003 Michigan affirmative action cases, while it upheld Michigan Law School's "holistic" admissions policy as narrowly tailored to satisfy the school's compelling interest in diversity among its students. In her court opinion in *Grutter v. Bollinger*, 539 U.S. 306, 326 (2003), Justice O'Connor asserted that "strict scrutiny is not 'strict in theory, but fatal in fact'" (citing *Adarand Constructors* at 237).

16. *Reed v. Reed*, 404 U.S. 71 (1971), and *Frontiero v. Richardson*, 411 U.S. 677 (1973)

17. In *Frontiero*, Justice Brennan tried, unsuccessfully to get the Court to find sex a "suspect classification." Justice Powell, who concurred in the result, said such a broad holding was not necessary to decide the case and that that very question was under consideration with the equal rights amendment, which was up for ratification (it failed to secure the necessary three-fourths of the states).

18. *Craig v. Boren*, 429 U.S. 190, 198 (1976). Justice Brennan thus implied that the Court had already introduced this new level of scrutiny, but he clearly came up one vote short in *Frontiero* from holding sex to be a suspect class, like race. Justice Stevens' reference to the Court's "two-tiered analysis" in the case recognizing a third, middle-tiered, test, is puzzling. Perhaps he was prescient in assuming that there would be little difference between strict and heightened scrutiny. At the time, laws restricting women in combat positions in the military were understood to pass constitutional muster under heightened but not strict scrutiny.

19. *Mississippi v. Hogan*, 458 U.S. 718 (1982); *United States v. Virginia*, 518 U.S. 515 (1996).

20. *Craig*, 429 U.S. at 211, 212.

21. *San Antonio v. Rodriguez*, 411 U.S. 1 (1973); *Dandridge v. Williams*, 397 U.S. 471 (1970).

22. 473 U.S. 432.

23. Id. at 440.

24. Id. at 440–41.

25. In addition, there is a range of disabilities, making a single strict standard inappropriate in all cases. Moreover, Justice White maintained that lawmakers have been responsive to the needs of the mentally retarded "in a manner that belies a continuing antipathy or prejudice and a corresponding need for more oversight by the judiciary." Id. at 442–43.

26. Id. at 453.

27. Id. at 458.

28. *Romer v. Evans*, 517 U.S. 620 (1996).

29. Id. at 632.

30. Id. at 635.

31. "The Supreme Court 1971 Term Foreword: In Search of Evolving Doctrine on a Changing Court: A Model for a Newer Equal Protection," 86 *Harv. L. Rev.* 1 (Nov. 1972) 18, 44, 47.

32. The Court's finding fundamental rights in the Due Process Clauses of the Fifth and Fourteenth Amendments goes back to two earlier and

related decisions: first, the limited reading the Court gave to the Fourteenth Amendment's Privileges and Immunities Clause in the *Slaughter House Cases*, 16 Wall 36 (1873); second, the subsequent reading of the concept of "ordered liberty" in the Due Process Clauses, in *Palko v. Connecticut*, 302 U.S. 319 (1937). The Court also has found a right to refuse treatment, in *Cruzan v. Missouri Dept. of Health*, 497 U.S. 261 (1990).

33. *Griswold v. Connecticut*, 381 U.S. 479 (1965).

34. See Justice Souter's concurring opinion in *Washington v. Glucksberg*, 521 U.S. 702, 762–3 (1997).

35. *Poe v. Ullman*, 367 U.S. 497 (1961).

36. Id. at 542.

37. Id. at 546–48. As much as Justice Harlan disagreed with Justice Douglas's approach to the Bill of Rights, his critical judgment on the law agreed with Douglas' rhetorical question in *Griswold*, "Would we allow the police to search the sacred precincts of marital bedrooms for telltale signs of the use of contraceptives?" *Griswold*, 381 U.S. at 485.

38. 405 U.S. 438.

39. 410 U.S. 113 (1973).

40. Id. at 153.

41. *Planned Parenthood v. Casey*, 505 U.S. 833, 851 (1992). Justice Kennedy employed similar grand language respecting liberty in his court opinions in *Lawrence v. Texas* and again in *Obergefell v. Hodges*.

42. *Lawrence*, 539 U.S. at 563.

43. 478 U.S. 186 (1986).

44. *Lawrence*, 539 U.S. at 567.

45. Id. at 569.

46. Id. at 571.

47. Id. at 572–73. Justice O'Connor, in her concurring opinion, suggested reliance on the Equal Protection Clause (since the law prohibited only homosexual sodomy), assuming, I believe, that the state would not have passed a more encompassing prohibition on sodomy, or if it did the law would not be enforced. I think she also thought that the more conservative equal protection approach would have made it more difficult for advocates of same-sex marriage to draw on this case for support. The difficulty with Justice O'Connor's approach is that if the state did pass an across the board prohibition on sodomy, without any intention of enforcing it, all homosexuals capable of sexual activity would have been stigmatized as potential lawbreakers.

48. Id. at 567, 578.

49. Id. at 585, 601.

50. Laurence Tribe, "*Lawrence v. Texas*: The 'Fundamental Right' that Dare Not Speak its Name," 117 *Harv. L. Rev.* 1893 (Apr. 2004) 1948.

51. *Loving v. Virginia*, 388 U.S. 1, 10 (1967). The Court could have cited *Bolling v. Sharpe* but did not.

52. Id. at 7.

53. Id. at 12.

54. Id.

55. Id.

56. *Skinner v. Oklahoma*, 316 U.S. 535, 541 (1942).

57. The Hawaii Supreme Court mentioned this when it rejected Plaintiffs' "right of privacy" argument as support for a fundamental right to marry. 74 Haw. 530, 552–53 (1993).

58. 434 U.S. 374 (1978).

59. Redhail acknowledged that he was the father of a child born out of wedlock; the child had been a public charge since her birth.

60. *Zablocki*, 434 U.S. 374 (1978); see Stewart's opinion at 393–94 and Powell's at 400.

61. "It is not surprising that the decision to marry has been placed on the same level of importance as decisions relating to procreation, childbirth, child rearing, and family relationships. . . . Surely a decision to marry and raise the child in a traditional family setting must receive equivalent protection [to the decision to abort an unwanted pregnancy]. And, if appellee's right to procreate means anything, it must imply some right to enter the only relationship in which the State of Wisconsin allows sexual relations legally to take place." 434 U.S. at 387.

62. 482 U.S. 78.

63. Id. at 96.

Chapter Five

1. *Baehr v. Lewin*, 852 P.2d 44 (Haw. 1993).

2. *Baker v. State*, 744 A.2d 864 (Vt. 1999).

3. *Goodridge v. Dept. of Public Health*, 798 N.E.2d 941 (Mass. 2003).

4. *Hernandez v. Robles*, 855 N.E.2d 1 (N.Y. 2006).

5. *Andersen v. King County*, 138 P.3d 963 (Wash. 2006).

6. *Lewis v. Harris*, 908 A.2d 196 (N.J. 2006).

7. *Conaway v. Deane*, 932 A.2d 571 (Md. 2007).

8. *In re Marriage Cases*, 183 P.3d 384 (Cal. 2008), superseded by constitutional amendment, Cal. Const. art. I, § 7.5 (2008), invalidated by *Perry v. Schwarzenegger*, 704 F. Supp. 2d 921, 927 (N.D. Cal. 2010).

9. *Kerrigan v. Commissioner of Public Health*, 957 A.2d 407 (Conn. 2008).

10. *Varnum v. Brien*, 763 N.W.2d 862 (Iowa 2009). I exclude the 1971 Minnesota case *Baker v. Nelson*, 191 N.W.2d 185, which I discussed previously, because it predates increased judicial scrutiny of issues related to same-sex marriage. In addition, the plaintiffs challenged the state marriage law solely on federal constitutional grounds; an independent state constitutional argument was not made. Id. at 186–87. In four other states—Kentucky (1973), Georgia (2002), Arizona (2003), and Indiana (2005)—the court of appeals decided against the same-sex marriage plaintiffs, and either an appeal was not taken or the highest state court refused to accept the appeal. *Standhardt v. Superior Court ex rel. County of Maricopa*, 77 P.3d 451 (Ct. App. Ariz. 2003); *Burns v. Burns*, 560 S.E.2d 47 (Ct. App. Ga. 2002); *Morrison v. Sadler*, 821 N.E.2d 15 (Ct. App. Ind. 2005); *Jones v. Hallahan*, 501 S.W.2d 588 (Ct. App. Ky. 1973). In addition, the District of Columbia Court of Appeals, the highest court in the District, handed down a decision against same-sex marriage in 1995, a year before the *Romer* decision in the U.S. Supreme Court. *Dean v. District of Columbia*, 653 A.2d 307 (D.C. 1995). However, in 2009 the mayor signed a bill passed by the Council of the District of Columbia legalizing same-sex marriage. Equal Access to Marriage, 46 D.C. Code § 46-401 (2010).

11. *Lewis*, 908 A.2d at 224; *Baker v. State*, 744 A.2d at 886.

12. *Marriage Cases*, 183 P.3d at 453; *Kerrigan*, 957 A.2d at 482; *Baehr*, 852 P.2d at 67; *Varnum*, 763 N.W.2d at 906–7; *Goodridge*, 798 N.E.2d at 968.

13. *Conaway*, 932 A.2d at 635; *Hernandez*, 855 N.E.2d at 12; *Andersen*, 138 P.3d at 990.

14. The margin was two votes in Vermont and New York and one vote in all the other states. This even included Hawaii; see *Baehr*, 852 P.2d at 48 (explaining that the formal vote to apply strict scrutiny was 3-to-1, but a judge whose temporary assignment to the court by reason of a vacancy expired before the opinion was filed indicated that he would have joined the dissent).

15. Haw. Const. art. I, § 23.

16. Cal. Const. art. I, § 7.5.

17. *Baehr*, 852 P.2d at 55, 58.

18. See id. at 55–57 (discussing the right of privacy claim).

19. The Hawaii Constitution's Equal Protection Clause reads: "[n]o person shall . . . be denied the equal protection of the laws, *nor be denied the enjoyment of the person's civil rights or be discriminated against in the exer-*

cise thereof because of race, religion, *sex or* ancestry." Haw. Const. art. 1, § 5 (emphases added).

20. *Baehr*, 852 P.2d at 67.

21. Id. at 68.

22. "Full faith and credit shall be given in each state to the public acts, records, and judicial proceedings of every other state. And the Congress may by general laws prescribe the manner in which such acts, records, and proceedings shall be proved, and the effect thereof." U.S. Const. art. 4, § 1.

23. "No State, territory, or possession of the United States, or Indian tribe, shall be required to give effect to any public act, record, or judicial proceeding of any other State, territory, possession, or tribe respecting a relationship between persons of the same sex that is treated as a marriage under the laws of such other State, territory, possession, or tribe, or a right or claim arising from such relationship." Defense of Marriage Act, Pub. L. 104-199, § 2(a), 110 Stat. 2419 (1996) (codified at 28 U.S.C. § 1738C (2012)).

"[T]he word 'marriage' means only a legal union between one man and one woman as husband and wife, and the word 'spouse' refers only to a person of the opposite sex who is a husband or a wife." DOMA § 3(a).

24. Haw. Const. art. 1, § 23.

25. *Baehr v. Miike*, No. 203 458 U.S. 457 (1982)71, 1999 WL 35643448, at 1 (Haw. Dec. 9, 1999).

26. 174 Vt. 194, 744 A.2d 864 (1999).

27. Id. at 197, 744 A.2d at 867. The relevant portion of the Vermont Constitution provides: "That government is, or ought to be, instituted for the common benefit, protection, and security of the people, nation, or community, and not for the particular emolument or advantage of any single person, family, or set of persons, who are a part only of that community." Vt. Const. ch. 1, art. VII.

28. *Baker v. State*, 744 A.2d. at 886. The court described this option as:

[W]hat are typically referred to as "domestic partnership" or "registered partnership" acts, which generally establish an alternative legal status to marriage for same-sex couples, impose similar formal requirements and limitations, create a parallel licensing or registration scheme, and extend all or most of the same rights and obligations provided by the law to married partners.

29. David Moats, *Civil Wars: A Battle for Gay Marriage* (Harcourt, 2004), 240–42.

30. *Baker v. State*, 744 A.2d at 876–78.

31. Id. at 871. Chief Justice Amestoy described Cass Sunstein as having "documented the United States Supreme Court's unacknowledged departures from the deferential rational-basis standard without defining a new kind of scrutiny." Id. at 872 n. 5 (citing Cass Sunstein, "The Supreme Court 1995 Term Foreword: Leaving Things Undecided," 110 *Harv. L. Rev.* 40, 59–61 (1996). He also referred to the Gunther article on equal protection, which I indicated introduced the kind of "rational basis with bite" scrutiny that Chief Justice Amestoy is applying here. Id. (citing Gunther, "The Supreme Court 1971 Term: Foreword: In Search of Evolving Doctrine on a Changing Court: A Model for a Newer Equal Protection," 86 *Harv. L. Rev.* 1, 8 (1972)). I refer to this article in chapter two—see text accompanying note 5; see also chapter 4, text accompanying note 31. Sunstein, surprisingly, did not refer to Gunther's 1972 *Harvard Law Review* article on the newer equal protection in his comparable *Harvard Law Review* article 24 years later. See Sunstein, "Leaving Things Undecided." Justice Dooley wrote separately to say that he objected to the Chief Justice's use of rational basis analysis and would have preferred some version of heightened scrutiny. *Baker v. State*, 744 A.2d at 889–93. Justice Johnson, in a partial concurrence and partial dissent, agreed with Justice Dooley that "some level of heightened scrutiny" was required. Id. at 907 (Johnson, J., concurring in part, dissenting in part). The justices were not that far apart. Of their positions, I favor Chief Justice Amestoy's because I think it results in a fairer balancing test.

32. *Baker v. State*, 744 A.2d at 881–82.

33. Id. (referring to same-sex couples that raise children and observing that "the statutes plainly exclude many same-sex couples who are no different from opposite-sex couples with respect to these objectives"). In this respect, the law could be described as over-inclusive as well as under-inclusive with respect to couples that are excluded.

34. Id. at 882.

35. Id.

36. Id.

37. Id. at 883.

38. Id. at 884–85.

39. See id. at 901–2 (Johnson, J., concurring in part, dissenting in part).

40. Id. at 886 (majority opinion).

41. Moats, *Civil Wars*, 240–42.

42. Vt. Stat. Ann. tit. 15, § 1204(a) (2010). The statement of benefits (§ 1204) reads as follows: "Parties to a civil union shall have all the same benefits, protections, and responsibilities under law, whether they

derive from statute, administrative or court rule, policy, common law, or any other source of civil law, as are granted to spouses in a civil marriage." See also *Baker v. State*, 744 A.2d at 883–84 (describing the state benefits of marriage).

43. Dave Gram, *Vermont Legalizes Gay Marriage, Overrides Governor's Veto*, Huffington Post (May 8, 2009), http://www.huffingtonpost.com/2009/04/07/vermont-legalizes-gay-mar_n_184034.html. The vote in the House of Representatives was 100-to-49, barely reaching the required two-thirds majority.

44. See Sunstein, "Leaving Things Undecided," 96–99, in which the author discusses how *Romer v. Evans* could be used to imply that state bans on same-sex marriage do not have a rational basis.

45. 798 N.E.2d 941 (Mass. 2003).

46. Id. at 969.

47. Id. at 961. The majority opinion notes that the plaintiffs challenged the state's marriage law on both equal protection and due process grounds and states: "Much of what we say concerning one standard applies to the other." Id. at 953, 960. The court "conclude[s] that the marriage ban does not meet the rational basis test for either due process or equal protection. Because the statute does not survive rational basis review, we do not consider the plaintiffs' arguments that this case merits strict judicial scrutiny." Id. at 961.

48. Id. at 970–72 (Greaney, J., concurring).

49. Id. at 974, 978, 983.

50. Id. at 948.

51. Id. Given the emphasis on benefits, it is surprising that no justice considered Vermont's "civil unions" resolution. Only after the decision was handed down and the state senate presented as a question of law whether an equal benefits approach would satisfy the state's constitution, did the Massachusetts Supreme Judicial Court consider the question. Opinions of the Justices to the Senate, 802 N.E.2d 565, 568 (2004). On the authority of *Goodridge*, the court, in a 5-to-2 vote with Justice Cordy writing the majority opinion, advised the senate that prohibiting same-sex couples from using the term "marriage" assigned such couples "to second-class status" and violated the state's constitution. 802 N.E.2d at 570. Since Justice Cordy dissented in *Goodridge*, he was clearly following the logical implications of that decision. Two justices continued to dissent, however. 802 N.E.2d at 565, 579, 581. The Massachusetts Supreme Court, unlike the U.S. Supreme Court, is authorized to issue "advisory opinions" on questions of law. Wex Legal Dictionary, *Advisory Opinion*, Cornell Univ. Law Sch., http://www.law.cornell.edu/wex/advisory_opinion (last visited Dec. 5, 2014).

52. *Goodridge*, 798 N.E.2d at 948.

53. Id. (quoting *Lawrence*, 539 U.S. 558, 571 (2003) (quoting *Planned Parenthood v. Casey*, 505 U.S. 833, 850 (1992)))).

54. *Goodridge*, 798 N.E.2d at 948.

55. Id. at 953.

56. Id.

57. Id. at 961–65.

58. Id. at 961.

59. See the text quoted at notes 8–12, chapter four.

60. *Goodridge*, 798 N.E.2d at 961.

61. In his review of Andrew Sullivan's *Virtually Normal*, James Q. Wilson responds to the analogy to sterile persons by affirming the importance of the form: "Yet people, I think, want the form observed even when the practice varies; a sterile marriage, whether from choice or necessity, remains a marriage of a man and a woman." Wilson, "Against Homosexual Marriage," 140. The argument regarding forms needs to be viewed in relation to an underlying argument in support of traditional marriage to be persuasive. If children are better off raised by their biological parents, or at least by a man and a woman, the right to marry need not be limited to heterosexual couples who are ready, willing, and able to procreate.

62. *Goodridge*, 798 N.E.2d at 962.

63. Id. at 963.

64. Id. at 979–80 (Sosman, J., dissenting); id. at 995 (Cordy, J., dissenting).

65. See id. at 962–63 (majority opinion).

66. Id. at 963.

67. Id. at 965.

68. Id. at 968.

69. Id. at 979 (Sosman, J., dissenting).

70. Id.

71. Id.

72. Id. at 966 (majority opinion) (quoting *United States v. Virginia*, 518 U.S. 515, 557 (1996)).

73. Id. at 968.

74. Id.

75. Id.

76. Id. at note 33.

77. 855 N.E.2d 1 (N.Y. 2006).

78. Id. at 22.

79. Id.

80. Id. (Kaye, C.J., dissenting).

81. Id. at 7 (majority opinion).

82. Id.

83. Id. at 8.

84. Id.

85. Id.

86. Id.

87. Id. at 9 (quoting *Washington v. Glucksberg*, 521 U.S. 702, 721 (1997) (quoting *Moore v. East Cleveland*, 431 U.S. 494, 503 (1977))).

88. Id. at 10. ("We conclude that, by defining marriage as it has, the New York Legislature has not restricted the exercise of a fundamental right.")

89. Id.

90. Id. at 10–11 (rejecting the contention that the law involved sex discrimination, since it does not put men and women in different classes and was not passed to subordinate women to men or vice versa).

91. Id. at 11 ("[N]o more than rational basis scrutiny is generally appropriate 'where individuals in the group affected by a law have distinguishing characteristics relevant to interests the State has the authority to implement.'" (quoting *Cleburne v. Cleburne Living Ctr.*, 473 U.S. 432, 441 (1985)))).

92. Id.

93. Id.

94. Id.

95. Id. at 11–12.

96. Id. at 22 (Kaye, C.J., dissenting).

97. Id. at 34.

98. *Marbury v. Madison*, 5 U.S. 137, 177 (1803); see also Federalist 78 (Alexander Hamilton) in Robert Scigliano, ed., *The Federalist* (Modern Library, 2001), 498. ("The interpretation of the law is the proper and peculiar province of the courts.")

99. Federalist 10 (James Madison) in Scigliano, 56. ("No man is allowed to be a judge in his own cause, because his interest would certainly bias his judgment, and, not improbably, corrupt his integrity. With equal, nay with greater reason, a body of men are unfit to be both judges and parties at the same time; yet what are many of the most important acts of legislation, but so many judicial determinations, not indeed concerning the rights of single persons but concerning the rights of large bodies of citizens?")

100. *Hernandez*, 855 N.E.2d at 23 (Kaye, C.J., dissenting) (quoting *Washington v. Glucksberg*, 521 U.S. 702, 721–22 (1997)). Chief Justice Rehnquist's remarks in *Glucksberg* drew on two due process opinions from the 1930s: *Snyder v. Massachusetts* and *Palko v. Connecticut*. See *Glucksberg*,

521 U.S. at 720–21 (quoting *Palko v. Connecticut*, 302 U.S. 319, 325, 326 (1937), *overruled by Benton v. Maryland*, 395 U.S. 784 (1969)) (citing *Snyder v. Massachusetts*, 291 U.S. 97, 105 (1934), *overruled in part by Malloy v. Hogan*, 378 U.S. 1 (1964)). Interestingly, Justice Rehnquist took issue with Justice Souter's formulation, in his concurrence, of the fundamental rights doctrine. See id. at 721–22. According to Justice Rehnquist, Justice Souter was wrong to follow Justice Harlan's *Poe v. Ullman* opinion, restated in *Griswold*, because it allowed for a more open-ended judicial scrutiny than the Court had ever endorsed. See id. But Justice Souter's account also relied on the *Snyder* language, repeated in *Palko*, emphasizing "'principles of justice so rooted in the traditions and conscience of our people as to be ranked as fundamental.'" Id. at 768 (Souter, J., concurring) (quoting *Palko*, 302 U.S. at 325 (quoting *Snyder*, 291 U.S. at 105)).

101. *Hernandez*, 855 N.E.2d at 23 (Kaye, C.J., dissenting).

102. See id. at 25 (explaining that under the state constitution, discriminatory views cannot stop same-sex couples from marrying any more than they could different-race couples).

103. See *Goodridge*, 798 N.E.2d at 971–72. ("The equal protection infirmity at work here is strikingly similar to (although, perhaps, more subtle than) the invidious discrimination perpetuated by Virginia's anti-miscegenation laws. . . .")

104. See *Hernandez*, 855 N.E.2d at 26 (Kaye, C.J., dissenting) (predicting that the opposition to same-sex marriage will fade away, as did the opposition to different-race marriage).

105. Id. at 27.

106. Id. at 27–28. Chief Judge Kaye also regards the state's marriage law as classifying by sex in not allowing same-sex couples to marry, and she restates the fundamental rights argument in the equal protection context. Id. at 27, 30.

107. Id. at 30.

108. Id.

109. *Lockyer v. City & Cnty. of San Francisco*, 95 P.3d 459, 499 (Cal. 2004).

110. *In re Marriage Cases*, 183 P.3d 384, 398 n. 2, 416–17 n. 24, (Cal. 2008), superseded by constitutional amendment, Cal. Const. art. I, § 7.5 (2008), invalidated by *Perry v. Schwarzenegger*, 704 F. Supp. 2d 921, 927 (N.D. Cal. 2010).

111. *Marriage Cases*, 183 P.3d at 398. While Chief Judge George does not explicitly refer to the California Constitution here, he clearly has in mind the first clause of article I, section 7, which reads: "A person may not be

deprived of life, liberty, or property without due process of law or denied equal protection of the laws. . . ." See California Legislative Information.

112. 183 P.3d at 399.

113. See Ronald Dworkin, *Taking Rights Seriously* (Harvard Univ. Press, 1977), 180–83, discussing the ideas of equal concern and respect in society in Rawls's *A Theory of Justice* (1971), 501, 272–78.

114. *Marriage Cases*, 183 P.3d at 457–58 (Baxter, J., dissenting).

115. Id. ("[T]he majority suggests that, by enacting *other statutes* which *do* provide substantial rights to gays and lesbians—including domestic partnership rights which, under [the initiative], the Legislature *could not call* 'marriage'—the Legislature has given 'explicit official recognition' to a California right of equal treatment which, because it includes the right to marry, thereby invalidates [the initiative]." (citations omitted) (quoting id. at 428 (majority opinion))).

116. Id. at 421 (majority opinion).

117. Id. at 427.

118. Id. at 428–29.

119. Id. at 427.

120. See id. at 428–29 (discussing the "change" in California's "past treatment of gay individuals and homosexual conduct").

121. See Richard Posner, *Sex and Reason*, 100–108, 291–93 (1992) (detailing homosexuality and genetics and challenges to homosexuals based on social policy).

122. *Marriage Cases*, 183 P.3d at 429.

123. Id. at 431 (citing *Baker v. Baker*, 13 Cal. 87, 103 (1859)); David Blankenhorn, *The Future of Marriage* (2007), 23–125.

124. *Marriage Cases*, 183 P.3d at 431.

125. Id. at 432–33.

126. The rest of the majority opinion explained: (1) for Equal Protection Clause purposes, the statutes discriminated on the basis of sexual orientation; (2) the statutes had to be subject to strict scrutiny, as California had a two-tier system, with no intermediate scrutiny and sexual orientation satisfied the requirements of heightened scrutiny; and (3) there was no compelling state interest "in limiting the designation of marriage exclusively to opposite-sex couples." See id. at 435–52. Since the majority had already concluded that the fundamental right to marry extended to same-sex couples, the only new part consisted of the unsurprising conclusion that the law limiting marriage to opposite-sex couples failed strict scrutiny. See id. at 443–52.

127. Id. at 456 (Baxter, J., concurring and dissenting); id. at 469–70 (Corrigan, J., concurring and dissenting).

128. Id. at 448 (majority opinion) (emphasis omitted).

Chapter Six

1. Debra Bowen, Cal. Sec'y of State, Statement of Vote: November 4, 2008, General Election 6–7 (2008), available at http://www.sos.ca.gov/elections/sov/2008-general/sov_complete.pdf.

2. See *Strauss v. Horton*, 207 P.3d 48, 59 (Cal. 2009) (quoting Cal. Const. art. I, § 7.5).

3. Id. at 68–69.

4. Amendments and revisions both require the vote of a majority of the people for ratification. But, an amendment may be proposed either by two-thirds of both houses of the legislature or by an initiative petition signed by a number of voters equal to at least 8 percent of the votes cast in the last election for governor, while a revision requires the vote of two-thirds of both houses. Cal. Const. art. XVIII, § 1; see also *Strauss*, 207 P.3d at 61–62 (discussing the difference between an amendment and a revision).

5. See *Strauss*, 207 P.3d at 65–66 (explaining how Proposition 22's language was used for Proposition 8).

6. Id. at 76. California Domestic Partner Rights and Responsibilities Act of 2003, ch. 421 § 4, 2003 Cal. Stat. 89, 89 (codified as amended at Cal. Fam. Code § 297.5 (West 2007)); see *Strauss*, 207 P.3d at 76. In addition, following precedent on retroactivity, the court interpreted the provision to be prospective only, and hence not to affect any same-sex couple that had been married in the year since the *Marriage Cases* decision. *Strauss*, 207 P.3d at 76. The court said they were doing this to avoid possible due process challenges concerning the taking away of vested rights. Id. at 121.

7. *Perry v. Schwarzenegger*, 704 F. Supp. 2d 921, 926–27 (N.D. Cal. 2010); see also *The Case Against 8* (HBO 2014) (showing the full account of the collaboration).

8. *Bush v. Gore*, 531 U.S. 98, 99 (2000). For their account of their role in the case, see David Boies and Theodore Olson, *Redeeming the Dream: The Case for Marriage Equality* (Viking, 2014). For both of these lawyers, *Loving v. Virginia* was the key precedent. See the index entry for that case.

9. *Perry v. Schwarzenegger*, 704 F. Supp. 2d 921, 926–27 (N.D. Cal. 2010); see also *The Case Against 8* (HBO 2014) (showing the full account of the collaboration).

10. See Chuleenan Svetvilas, *Challenging Prop. 8: The Hidden Story: How Activists Filed a Federal Lawsuit to Overturn California's Same-Sex Marriage Ban*, Daily J. Corp. (Jan. 2010), http://www.callawyer.com/Clstory.cfm?eid=906575 (chronicling the decision to challenge Proposition 8 in federal court, including conservative lawyer Ted Olson persuading liberal lawyer David Boies to join him on the brief).

11. *Perry*, 704 F. Supp. 2d at 921, 1004.

12. Id. at 929.

13. Id. at 930.

14. Id. (emphasis omitted) (quoting Ron Prentice et. al, "Argument in Favor of Proposition 8," in California General Election Tuesday, November 4, 2008 Official Voter Information Guide 56, available at http://librarysource.uchastings.edu/ballot_pdf/2008g.pdf).

15. Id. at 993.

16. Id. at 931, 945.

17. Id. at 960, 979.

18. Id. at 931 (internal quotation marks omitted). In his preface to Blankenhorn's *Future of Marriage*, Jonathan Rauch posed a similar question (xi, xiii–xix, critiquing Blankenhorn's arguments against same-sex marriage).

19. *Perry*, 704 F. Supp. 2d at 934. Blankenhorn consistently acknowledged that there would be benefits to same-sex couples who wished to have and raise children; but, initially he thought that the resulting harm to marriage as an institution, and hence to a larger number of children, outweighed the benefit to same-sex couples with children. For his change of mind on this important political question, see "How My View on Gay Marriage Has Changed," *New York Times*, June 22, 2012 ("[I]f fighting gay marriage was going to help marriage over all, I think we'd have seen some signs of it by now").

20. *Perry*, 704 F. Supp. 2d at 932.

21. Id. at 933–34.

22. Id. at 933.

23. Id.

24. Id. at 934, 938.

25. Id. at 934. Judge Walker discusses the trial evidence in points 19 through 41 of his Findings of Fact. See id. at 956–63 (discussing whether there is evidence supporting California's refusal to recognize same-sex marriage).

26. See id. at 958–59 (discussing racial restrictions on marriage and division of family labor based on gender in points 25 through 27).

27. Id. at 935.

28. Id.

29. Id.

30. Id.

31. Id.

32. Id.

33. Id. at 936–38.

34. Id. at 937.

35. Id. at 938.

36. Id. at 991–93.

37. Id. at 992.

38. Id. at 992–93.

39. Id. at 992.

40. See id. at 993 ("[T]he exclusion [of same-sex couples from marriage] exists as an artifact of a time when the genders were seen as having distinct roles in society and in marriage. That time has passed.").

41. Id. at 943. When he testified, Lamb, head of the Department of Social and Developmental Psychology at Cambridge University, identified himself as a long-time researcher of issues concerning children's social and emotional development. See Transcript of Proceedings at 1004, *Perry v. Schwarzenegger*, 704 F. Supp. 2d 921 (2010) (No. C 09-2292-VRW), available at http://www.afer.org/wp-content/uploads/2010/01/Perry-Vol-5-1-15-10.pdf. His testimony drew on a review of hundreds of studies of children being raised by gay and lesbian parents. Id. at 1005–8. Lamb subsequently published a summary of those studies. Michael Lamb, "Mothers, Fathers, Families and Circumstances: Factors Affecting Children's Adjustment," 16 *Applied Developmental Sci.* 98, 98–99 (2012).

42. See Transcript of Proceedings at 1009–10, *Perry*, 704 F. Supp. 2d 921 (describing Dr. Lamb's broad opinions on the adjustment of children raised by gay and lesbian parents). Lamb began his testimony by defining a well-adjusted child as one "who had no significant behavioral or psychological problems," who could "interact effectively" with others and perform well in school. Id. at 1004–5; see also Lamb, "Mothers, Fathers, Families and Circumstances" at 99, 102, 104. ("Well-adjusted individuals have sufficient social skills to get along with others (at school, in social settings, and at work), to get along and comply with rules and authority, to function well at school and in the workplace, and to establish and maintain meaningful intimate relationships.")

43. Id. at 1010–11.

44. See id. at 1058–1124, 1129–84 (transcribing Attorney Thompson's cross-examination on these points).

45. See id. (transcribing Attorney Thompson's cross examination); id. at 1185–1207 (transcribing Attorney McGill's redirect).

46. Id. at 1053–54.

47. Id. at 1184.

48. Brief for Leon R. Kass et al. as Amici Curiae Supporting Petitioners at 3–4, 17–18, *Hollingsworth v. Perry*, 133 S. Ct. 2652 (2013) (No. 12-144). Mansfield has stated that Nelson Lund, counsel of record, wrote the amicus brief. Email from Harvey Mansfield, Professor of Government, Harvard University, to Murray Dry, Professor of Political Science, Middlebury College (Sept. 3, 2014) (on file with author).

49. See id. at 31 (noting challenges with producing evidence to support either side of the same-sex marriage debate).

50. Amy Wax, "The Conservative's Dilemma," 42 *San Diego L. Rev.* 1059.

51. Id. at 1099.

52. Id. at 1101–3.

53. *Perry v. Brown*, 671 F.3d 1052, 1064 (9th Cir. 2012), vacated and remanded sub nom. *Hollingsworth v. Perry*, 133 S. Ct. 786 (2012).

54. Id. at 1076 (citing *Romer v. Evans*, 517 U.S. 620, 634–35 (1996)).

55. Id. at 1104 (Smith, J., dissenting).

56. Id. at 1080 (majority opinion).

57. Id. at 1090.

58. Id. at 1102–5 (Smith, J., dissenting).

59. Id. at 1104–12.

60. Id. at 1110.

61. Id. at 1108.

62. Id. at 1111.

64. Id. at 1096. In June of 2012, the Ninth Circuit denied Proposition 8 supporters' motion to rehear the case en banc. *Perry v. Brown*, 681 F.3d 1065, 1066 (9th Cir. 2012); see also Doug Mataconis, *Ninth Circuit Declines En Banc Review of Proposition 8 Decision*, Outside the Beltway (June 5, 2012), http://www.outsidethebeltway.com/ninth-circuit-declines-en-banc-review-of-proposition-8-decision/. The supporters of Proposition 8 sought Supreme Court review on July 31, 2012. American Foundation for Equal Rights, *U.S. Supreme Court Asked to Hear Prop. 8 Case*, Marriage News Blog (July 31, 2012), http://www.afer.org/blog/u-s-supreme-court-asked-to-hear-prop-8-case/.

64. *Hollingsworth v. Perry*, 133 S. Ct. 2652 (2013), discussed below.

65. DOMA, Pub. L. 104–199, §§ 2(a), 3(a), 110 Stat. 2419 (1996) (codified at 1 U.S.C. § 7 (2012), 28 U.S.C. § 1738(c) (2012)).

66. DOMA § 2(a), 28 U.S.C. § 1738(c) (2012).

67. DOMA § 3(a), 1 U.S.C. § 7 (2012), invalidated by *United States v. Windsor*, 133 S. Ct. 2675 (2013).

68. *Windsor v. United States*, 833 F. Supp. 2d 394, 397 (S.D.N.Y. 2012), aff'd, 699 F.3d 169 (2d Cir. 2012), aff'd, 133 S. Ct. 2675 (2013).

69. Id.

70. Id. at 398–99.

71. Id. at 397.

72. Id. at 401, 406 (citing *City of Cleburne v. Cleburne Living Ctr.*, 473 U.S. at 441).

73. Id. at 403–05.

74. See DOMA, Pub. L. 104-199, § 3(a), 110 Stat. 2419 (1996) (codified at 1 U.S.C. § 7 (2012)), invalidated by *United States v. Windsor*, 133 S. Ct. 2675 (2013).

75. Id.

76. See *Windsor*, 833 F. Supp. 2d at 405–6 (noting that "DOMA operates to reexamine the states' decisions concerning same-sex marriage" not to actually define any particular requirements for marriage).

77. *Windsor v. United States*, 699 F.3d 169, 181–85 (2d Cir. 2012), aff'd, 133 S. Ct. 2675 (2013). The major case is *Cleburne*, in which the Court struck down a zoning regulation without concluding that mental retardation merited heightened scrutiny. *City of Cleburne*, 473 U.S. at 435.

78. *Windsor*, 699 F.3d at 185.

79. *Hollingsworth v. Perry*, 133 S. Ct. 2652, 2652 (2013); *United States v. Windsor*, 133 S. Ct. at 2675.

80. *Hollingsworth*, 133 S. Ct. at 2659, 2668.

81. Id. at 2659.

82. *Windsor*, 133 S. Ct. at 2675, 2680.

83. Id. at 2681.

84. Id. at 2696 (Roberts, C.J., dissenting); Id. at 2697 (Scalia, J., dissenting); Id. at 2711 (Alito, J., dissenting). Justice Alito agreed with the majority in finding that BLAG had standing, so his dissent was limited to the merits. Id. at 2712, 2714 (Alito, J., dissenting). The other dissenting justices disagreed with both the standing decision and the decision on the merits. Id. at 2696 (Roberts, C.J., dissenting); Id. at 2697 (Scalia, J., dissenting).

85. Id. at 2689 (majority opinion).

86. Id. at 2689–90.

87. Id. at 2692.

88. Id.

89. Id. at 2693.

90. Id. at 2694 (citation omitted).

91. Id. at 2695.
92. DOMA, Pub. L. 104-199, § 2(a), 110 Stat. 2419 (1996) (codified at 28 U.S.C. § 1738(c) (2012)).
93. *Windsor*, 133 S. Ct. at 2694.
94. See my discussion of the lower federal courts' use of *Windsor*, in sec. F, beginning on p. 97.
95. *Windsor*, 133 S. Ct. at 2707 (Scalia, J., dissenting) (citation omitted).
96. Id. at 2718 (Alito, J., dissenting).
97. Id. at 2696 (Roberts, C.J., dissenting) (quoting id. at 2694 (majority opinion)). Kennedy actually wrote that DOMA's "principal purpose is to impose inequality." Id. at 2694 (majority opinion).
98. See id. (Roberts, C.J. dissenting) ("The Court does not have before it, and the logic of its opinion does not decide, the distinct question whether the States . . . may continue to utilize the traditional definition of marriage.").
99. Id. (quoting majority opinion).
100. Id. at 2696–97 (quoting id. at 2709 (Scalia, J. dissenting)).
101. Id. at 2697.
102. Id. at 2709–10 (Scalia, J., dissenting) (quoting id. at 2694 (majority opinion)). For example, Justice Scalia substituted "*[t]his state's law*" for "DOMA" and "*constitutionally protected sexual relationships*" for "state sanctioned marriages" in his first example. Id. at 2709.
103. Justice Kennedy did dissent from the Court's decision to deny that the proponents of Proposition 8 had standing in *Hollingsworth v. Perry*, 133 S. Ct. 2652, decided on June 26, 2013. Does that mean that Justice Kennedy was prepared to affirm that the Constitution prohibited states from denying same-sex marriage in 2013?
104. Lambda Legal, "Favorable Rulings in Marriage Equality Cases Since *U.S. v. Windsor*, as of June 24, 2015," www.lambdalegal.org/sites/default/files/post-windsor_cases_ruling_in_favor_of_marriage_equality_claims_as_of_6.24.2015.pdf.
105. These decisions were handed down by the Tenth Circuit on June 25, 2014 (*Kitchen v. Herbert*, 755 F.3d 1193), the Fourth Circuit on July 28, 2014 (*Bostic v. Schaefer*, 760 F.3d 352), the Seventh Circuit on September 4, 2014 (*Baskin v. Bogan*, 766 F.3d 648), and the Ninth Circuit on October 7, 2014 (*Latta v. Otter*, 771 F.3d 456).
106. *DeBoer v. Snyder*, 973 F. Supp. 2d 757 (E.D. Mich. 2014); *Obergefell v. Wymyslo*, 962 F. Supp. 2d 968 (S.D. Ohio 2013); *Henry v. Himes*, 14 F. Supp. 3d 1036 (S.D. Ohio 2014); *Bourke v. Beshear*, 996 F. Supp. 2d 542 (W.D. Ky. 2014); *Tanco v. Haslam*, 7 F. Supp. 3d 759 (M.D. Tenn. 2014); and

Love v. Beshear, 989 F. Supp. 2d 536 (W.D. Ky. 2014). The appeals in these cases were consolidated and decided on November 6, 2014, in *DeBoer v. Snyder*, 772 F.3d 388, in which the Sixth Circuit ruled that states could ban same-sex marriage.

107. *Baker v. Nelson*, 409 U.S. 810 (1972).

108. *Washington v. Glucksberg*, 521 U.S. 702 (1997).

109. *Kitchen v. Herbert*, 961 F. Supp. 2d 1181, 1203 (Utah 2013) (quoting from *Lawrence v. Texas*, 539 U.S. at 578–79). Justice Kennedy presents a comparable statement in his *Obergefell* opinion.

110. *Kitchen*, 961 F. Supp. 2d at 1203. Judge Lucero quoted the part about changing attitudes towards gay relationships in his court opinion in the Tenth Circuit's affirmation of the district court's decision; see *Kitchen v. Herbert*, 755 F.3d 1193, 1218 (2014).

111. While Judge Reinhardt was able to cite a case in which the Ninth Circuit interpreted the Supreme Court's *Windsor* decision to amount to a finding that sexual orientation classifications require heightened scrutiny, Judge Posner simply affirmed that position without a clear precedent from his circuit, although he later cited the Ninth Circuit's decision which interpreted the Supreme Court's *Windsor* decision to have implied as much. For Judge Reinhardt's reference to the *Smith Kline* decision, see text accompanying note 116, below.

112. *Baskin*, 766 F.3d at 654, 657.

113. Id. at 669.

114. Id. at 670.

115. Id. at 671–72. Interestingly, Judge Posner was not always of the view that the Constitution required same-sex marriage. As recently as in 2005, his writing reflected deference to majority sentiment. Even then however, he expressed his own view that a private contract approach to marriage was superior to having government regulate the institution. See The Becker-Posner Blog, July 17, 2005 "The Law and Economics of Gay Marriage," by Posner.

116. *Latta*, 771 F.3d at 464. "*Windsor* requires that heightened scrutiny be applied to equal protection claims involving sexual orientation" (quoting *SmithKline Beecham Corp. v. Abbott Laboratories*, 740 F.3d 471, 481 (9th Cir. 2014)).

117. See id. at 473–74.

118. *DeBoer v. Snyder*, 772 F.3d 388 (6th Cir. 2014).

119. Id. at 396.

120. *West Virginia State Board of Education v. Barnette*, 319 U.S. 624, 638 (1943). Judge Lucero quotes it in his *Kitchen* opinion, 755 F.3d at 1228.

121. *DeBoer*, 772 F.3d at 421.

122. Id. at 435.

123. Id. at 432–33, quoting Reva Siegel, "'The Rule of Love': Wife Beating as Prerogative and Privacy," 105 *Yale L.J.* 2117, 2125 (1996).

124. Id. at 416 (emphasis in original).

125. Id. at 434 (quoting from *Baskin*, 766 F.3d at 656).

126. Id. at 421 (Daughtrey, J. dissenting).

127. See my discussion in chapter five.

128. *Baker v. Nelson*, 409 U.S. 810 (1972).

129. *Romer v. Evans*, 517 U.S. 620 (1996) and *Lawrence v. Texas*, 539 U.S. 558 (2003).

130. *Windsor*, 133 S. Ct. at 2694.

131. See id. at 2682–96 (failing to discuss § 2 of DOMA).

132. DOMA, Pub. L. No. 104-199, § 2(a), 110 Stat. 2419 (1996) (codified at 28 U.S.C. § 1738(c) (2012)).

133. See, e.g., *DeBoer v. Snyder*, 973 F. Supp. 2d 757, 760, 772, 774 (E.D. Mich. 2014) (discussing DOMA § 3 but not § 2); *De Leon v. Perry*, 975 F. Supp. 2d 632, 661 (W.D. Tex. 2014) (mentioning DOMA § 2 only briefly in stating defendants' argument).

134. See, e.g., *DeBoer*, 973 F. Supp. 2d at 759 (stating Plaintiffs' equal protection and due process arguments); *De Leon*, 975 F. Supp. 2d at 656, 649–50 (noting equal protection and due process arguments).

135. See *Kitchen v. Herbert*, 755 F.3d 1193 1224-25 (10th Cir. 2014) (describing the state's lack of a narrowly tailored interest).

136. See the Lambda Legal data, cited previously, "Favorable Rulings in Marriage Equality Cases Since *U.S. v. Windsor*, as of June 24, 2015," www.lambdalegal.org/sites/default/files/post-windsor_cases_ruling_in_favor_of_marriage_equality_claims_as_of_6.24.2015.pdf.

137. See 521 U.S. 702, 721–22 (adopting a more conservative approach regarding fundamental rights).

Chapter Seven

1. The Sixth Circuit decided six cases that came from four states. The first petitioner with a writ of certiorari was Obergefell; hence the name of the case that reached the Supreme Court is *Obergefell v. Hodges*.

2. www.scotusblog.com for *Obergefell v. Hodges*, entry for July 16, 2015.

3. Oral argument on the first question arose out of the Michigan case, known as *DeBoer v. Snyder* in its certiorari petition and brief before the Su-

preme Court. Hence I will describe the arguments presented in this brief. The docket number for this case in the Supreme Court is 14-571. Scotus-blog.com provides all of the briefs of cases coming before the Supreme Court on its site. For some reason, however, I could not access Plaintiffs' brief in this case from that site. I located it on the University of Michigan Law School's Civil Rights Litigation Clearing House site.

4. *DeBoer* Petitioners' Brief, p. 30, in outline II.A. Petitioners followed this with the contention that sexual orientation classifications merited heightened scrutiny, and they concluded by making the Due Process Clause argument regarding the fundamental right to marry.

5. Id.

6. Id. at 32–33.

7. Id. at 34 (emphasis in original).

8. Id. at 45, from subheading 3.; see also p. 46 ("An examination of the text . . .").

9. Id. at 48.

10. See *DeBoer* Respondents' Brief, p. 8.

11. Id. at 10.

12. Id. at 11.

13. Id. at 13–14.

14. See Justice Kennedy's court opinion in *Obergefell v. Hodges*, 135 S. Ct. at 2597.

15. See Chief Justice Roberts's dissent in id. at 2611.

16. Oral argument in *Obergefell*, Docket 14-556, p. 29.

17. Respondents' Brief, p. 16.

18. Id. at 12.

19. Id. at 18; see also p. 26.

20. Respondents' Brief, p. 18.

21. See *Obergefell*, 135 S. Ct. at 2597.

22. Respondents' Brief, p. 41.

23. Id. at 43.

24. *Heller v. Doe*, 509 U.S. 312, 320 (1993), cited in *DeBoer* Respondents' Brief, pp. 30, 36–37, 42.

25. *Heller*, 509 U.S. at 319.

26. *DeBoer* Petitioners' Reply Brief, p. 2.

27. See my discussion in chapter 5.

28. *DeBoer* Petitioners' Reply Brief, p. 10.

29. Brief for United States, p. 3. (The United States submitted one amicus brief for all four cases coming out of the Sixth Circuit.) See also

pp. 27 and 29, where citations to U.S. Census Reports are given. The U.S. Census Bureau's Same-Sex Couple Household survey issued September 2011 reports that there were approximately 594,000 same sex couples in 2010 and that 115,000 reported having children. A comparable survey for 2013 reports 726,600 same-sex couples. That table does not provide information about children. The estimate is provided in the Brief. But another Census Report from 2011 puts the number of same-sex couples at 605,472 with 16 percent having children in the household (10 percent for male-male couples, 22 percent for female-female couples). These tables were issued in August 2013. The 16 percent figure compares with a 60 percent figure for opposite-sex couples. See U.S. Census, Families and Living Arrangements 2014 Family Households.

30. Brief for United States, p. 17. Most of this account came from the Court's *Cleburne* case, in which it declined to add "mental retardation" to the list of quasi-suspect classifications, while it decided with the group that challenged a refusal to grant a zoning variance for a group home for the mentally retarded. See *Cleburne*, 473 U.S. 432.

31. Brief for United States, p. 22.

32. Some would say that the Court has veered away from strict scrutiny in its treatment of race-based affirmative action. The means-end fit requirement has shifted from "no alternative means" to "narrowly tailored" means. And the "compelling interest" in diversity for the sake of education has been accepted, once schools assert it.

33. "Now the reason I'm interested in [the fundamental right to marry] is we don't get into this more scholastic effort to distinguish between rational basis and middle-tier and some higher tier and so forth." Justice Breyer, Oral Argument on question one, Docket 14-556, p. 59.

34. I draw on part of Justice Scalia's account of why the Court scrutinizes content-based legislation carefully, to avoid "the possibility that official suppression of ideas is afoot." See *R.A.V. v. St. Paul*, 505 U.S. 377, 390 (1992). The comparable statement about "suspect classifications" is the *Cleburne* Court's statement that classifications such as race, alienage, or national origin "are so seldom relevant to the achievement of any legitimate state interest that laws grounded in such considerations are deemed to reflect prejudice and antipathy" and are therefore subject to strict scrutiny. *Cleburne*, 473 U.S. at 440. See also *City of Richmond v. Croson*, 488 U.S. 469, 472 (1989) (the fit must be so close "that there is little or no possibility that the motive for the classification was illegitimate racial prejudice or stereotype.").

35. Oral argument, Docket 14-556, p. 4.

36. Id. at 5.

37. Id. at 6, 10 ("the man decided where the couple would be domiciled; it was her obligation to follow him").

38. Id. at 6–7.

39. Id. at 7.

40. Id. at 8.

41. Id. at 9.

42. Id. at 9.

43. Id. at 9–10.

44. Id. at 10–11.

45. Id. at 16.

46. Id. at 17.

47. Id. at 42–43.

48. Id. at 43.

49. Id. at 51.

50. Id. at 46.

51. Id. at 61–62.

52. Id. at 62 (citing *Nguyen v. INS*, 533 U.S. 53 (2001)).

53. Id. at 23–26.

54. Id. at 38.

55. Every justice save Justice Thomas has accepted the position that the Due Process Clauses contain a "substantive" liberty as well as procedural liberties.

56. *Washington v. Glucksberg*, 521 U.S. 702 (1997).

57. *Romer v. Evans*, 517 U.S. 620 (1996).

58. 135 S.Ct. 2584 at 2593.

59. *Washington v. Glucksberg*, 521 U.S. at 720 (internal citations omitted), quoted in part in Chief Justice Roberts's dissent in *Obergefell*, 135 S.Ct. at 2616. The Chief Justice then quoted from a 1986 address of then–circuit court judge Kennedy: "[I]t does not follow that each of those essential rights [in any just society] is one that we as judges can enforce under the written Constitution." Address at Stanford, 1986, p. 13, quoted at 2616.

60. In *Glucksberg*, the Court upheld the state of Washington's law against physician assisted suicide, distinguishing it from the right to refuse treatment, which the Court upheld in *Cruzan v. Missouri Dept. of Health*, 497 U.S. 261 (1990).

61. *Obergefell*, 135 S.Ct at 2613 (Roberts, C.J., dissenting) (quoting Cicero, *De Officiis*, § 54, ed. and trans. Walter Miller (Harvard Univ. Press, 1913)). The Chief Justice mistakenly identifies the passage as § 57.

62. *Obergefell*, 135 S. Ct at 2594 (quoting Cicero, *De Officiis*, § 54, (misidentified as 57)). Also the translation is different from the one cited. I

assume that Justice Kennedy decided to use Cicero on marriage and when the Chief Justice saw a draft of the court opinion and checked the source, he decided to provide the entire sentence. Cicero goes on in that section to mention "the foundation of civil government," and in section 57 he puts allegiance to country above all. "But when with a rational spirit you have surveyed the whole field, there is no social relation among them all more close, none more dear than that which links each one of us with our country. Parents are dear; dear are children, relatives, friends; but one native land embraces all our loves; and who that is true would hesitate to give his life for her, if by his death he could render her a service?"

63. Id.

64. Id. at 2598.

65. See Justice Scalia's dissent at id. at 2628–29 and Chief Justice Roberts's dissent at 2620–21.

66. Id. at 2599.

67. Id.

68. Id. at 2600.

69. Id. at 2601.

70. The four justices who joined in the court opinion chose not to write any concurring opinions. Justice Breyer, for example, would have put his emphasis elsewhere, I believe.

71. The Court had presumably rejected this approach in *West Coast Hotel v. Parrish*, 300 U.S. 379 (1937).

72. *Obergefell*, 135 S.Ct. at 2616.

73. Id. "There is after all, no 'Companionship and Understanding' or 'Nobility and Dignity' Clause in the Constitution."

74. Id. at 2622. The passage in Holmes's *Lochner* dissent that Chief Justice Roberts quoted earlier says the Constitution "is made for people of fundamentally differing views." In a later case, Holmes wrote an opinion holding that a state law restricting coal that could be mined from underground constituted a "taking" that required compensation. *Pennsylvania Coal Co. v. Mahon*, 260 U.S. 393 (1922). The Constitution apparently sets some limits on the scope of fundamental disagreements.

75. The logical extension of this argument would be to require federal benefits of the same kind for civil unions or domestic partnerships.

76. Justice Scalia allowed himself one acerbic remark, see *Obergefell*, 135 S.Ct. at 2630 (n. 22).

77. Id. at 2631. He did not discuss how he would address such questions under a revived privileges and immunities clause, which he has advocated

in other cases. See especially Justice Thomas's dissent in *McDonald v. Chicago*, 561 U.S. 742 (2010).

78. *Obergefell*, 135 S.Ct. at 2636 (Scalia, J., dissenting).

79. *Lawrence v. Texas*, 539 U.S. at 609.

80. *Obergefell*, 135 S. Ct. at 2642 (Alito, J., dissenting).

81. "*Baker v. Nelson* must be and now is overruled, and the State laws challenged by Petitioners in these cases are now held invalid to the extent they exclude same-sex couples from civil marriage on the same terms and conditions as opposite-sex couples." Id. at 2605.

82. *Washington v. Glucksberg*, 521 U.S. at 721.

83. Id. at 768.

84. At least with respect to the right of intimate association; cf. *Lawrence v. Texas*.

85. This is how one constitutional scholar framed the issue after the Court's decisions in *Lawrence* and *Windsor*, correctly predicting how Justice Kennedy would vote in *Obergefell*.

86. See the references in nn. 76–79 in this chapter.

87. See Jack Balkin's blog, Balkinization, "Living Originalism and Same-Sex Marriage," April 7, 2015; Ronald K. L. Collins, "Posner on Same-Sex Marriage: Then and Now," in concurringopinions.com, December 22, 2014. In his July 17, 2005 blog, Judge Posner wrote that the concern about same-sex marriage, in contrast to benefits that could have been secured via civil unions or domestic partnerships, was not significant enough to disturb public opinion. But later on, as more states, usually through their courts but sometimes through their legislatures required or allowed same-sex marriage, Judge Posner's position changed. In fairness to Judge Posner, as a "Millian" libertarian he was never impressed with the case for a government limitation on marriage. It was not surprising, then, that he should change his views on the subject and public opinion changed (see his May 13, 2012 blog and his *Baskin* opinion, discussed above). But that means that Judge Posner views the courts as not significantly different from legislatures, except for the need to be careful so as not to provoke a popular backlash.

88. See Marty Lederman's comments on *Obergefell* in "Supreme Court Breakfast Table," July 2, 2015, at slate.com. See also my discussion at p. 123 and note 93.

89. Balkinization (blog), "Living Originalism and Same-Sex Marriage," April 7, 2015.

90. Shortly after the Court decided *Lawrence*, Laurence Tribe wrote a law review article interpreting the decision to lead to a same-sex mar-

riage decision. See "*Lawrence v. Texas*: The 'Fundamental Right' that Dare Not Speak its Name," 117 *Harv. L. Rev.* 1893 (Apr. 2004). Cass Sunstein, who has written on homosexuality and the Constitution for over twenty years, has argued both that the "anti-caste" view of the Fourteenth Amendment points toward treating restrictions on same-sex marriage as similar to restrictions on interracial marriage ("Homosexuality and the Constitution", 70 *Ind. L.J.* 1 (1994) and for a more cautious approach to the constitutional question ("Liberty After Lawrence," 65 *Ohio St. L.J.* 1059 (2004), even though he wrote: "If *Lawrence* is put together with *Loving* and *Zablocki*, it might seem clear that the government would have to produce a compelling justification for refusing to recognize such marriages, and compelling justifications are not easy to find." Id. at 1078. The reason for Sunstein's caution then, and his embrace of the *Obergefell* decision when it came out (see "Gay Marriage Shows Court at its Best," *Bloomberg View*, 26 June 2015) is that he did not think that the Court should get ahead of public opinion (65 *Ohio St. L.J.* at 1075, 1079). Michael Klarman elaborates on that view in his 2015 law review article "*Windsor* and *Brown*: Marriage Equality And Racial Equality," 127 *Harv. Law R.* 127 (2013). Likewise, after the *Obergefell* decision was handed down, Jack Balkin, author of *Living Originalism*, wrote a blog drawing on the equality principle to support the decision. In a post on April 7, 2015, Balkin illustrated his understanding of originalism this way: "It follows, then, that we should ask what the principles of class legislation, caste legislation, and equality before the law mean in practice in today's world in the context of gays and lesbians who seek the right to marry."

91. Cass Sunstein, *One Case at a Time: Judicial Minimalism on the Supreme Court* (Harvard Univ. Press, 2001).

92. See nn. 90 and 91 immediately above.

93. "The Remarkable Disappearance of State Justifications in *Obergefell*," Balkinization, July 3, 2015, https://balkin.blogspot.com.

94. See Brief of American Pediatric Association.

95. Amy Wax, "The Conservative's Dilemma," 42 *San Diego L. Rev.* 1059.

Chapter Eight

1. See *Roe v. Wade*, 410 U.S. 113 (1973), and *Doe v. Bolton*, 410 U.S. 179 (1973). In *Roe*, the Texas law proscribed as criminal any abortion unless it was necessary to save the pregnant woman's life. In *Doe*, the Georgia law allowed abortion if in the best clinical judgment of the physician giving birth would "injure [the woman's] health; the fetus would likely be born

with a serious defect; or the pregnancy resulted from rape." In addition, a hospital staff abortion committee and two other licensed physicians had to agree with the performing physician's judgment (410 U.S. 179 syllabus). Given the scope of the Court's holding of the privacy-autonomy right in *Roe*, it is not surprising that the same majority struck down the more moderate Georgia law. Dissenting Justices White and Rehnquist apparently saw no reason for acknowledging the possible constitutional difference between the two laws. See 410 U.S. at 221. For the view that the Court both went too far in its *Roe* decision and that it should have employed an equal protection of the laws approach see Ruth B. Ginsburg, "Some Thoughts on Autonomy and Equality in Relation to *Roe v. Wade*," 63 *N.C. L. Rev.* 375 (1985).

2. Full comparability of benefits would have required the equivalent of a federal law granting the same federal benefits to state couples in a civil union.

3. 134 S.Ct. 1623 (2014).

4. Justice Sotomayor wrote a spirited dissent, which Justice Ginsburg joined. Part of the opinion objected to the way the policy was changed, as the referendum took the issue away from the universities' trustees. But part of it discussed the history of racial discrimination in the United States as if to suggest that affirmative action is a required, not simply a permissible, remedy for past discrimination.

5. See *Fisher v. University of Texas at Austin*, 136 S. Ct. 2198 (2016).

6. 558 U.S. 310 (2010).

7. In *SpeechNow.org v. Federal Election Commission*, 599 F.3d. 686 (D.C. Cir. 2010), the D.C. circuit court unanimously held that individuals and corporations may make unlimited contributions to groups that make independent expenditures. The Supreme Court denied cert on November 1, 2010, www.scotusblog.com.

8. 554 U.S. 570 (2008). Two years later, the Court held the second amendment right fully applicable to the states in *McDonald v. City of Chicago*, 561 U.S. 742 (2010).

9. Wilkinson, *Cosmic Constitutional Theory*, 57.

10. *Kelo v. City of New London*, 545 U.S. 469 (2005).

11. This included Senator Herb Kohl (D-WI), who expressed his dissatisfaction with the *Kelo* decision during the senate confirmation hearings for Samuel Alito (see Senate Confirmation Hearings of Samuel Alito, January 12, 2006).

12. A press release from the American Conservative Union decried the opinion: "**It is outrageous to think that the government can take away**

your home any time it wants to build a shopping mall," said ACU Chairman David Keene. "Today's Supreme Court ruling is a slap in the face to property owners everywhere . . . Liberal, activist judges will continue to violate the rights of individuals in favor of big government and special interests," continued Keene. "To help protect property rights, Americans must push for a fair, originalist judge to be appointed to the Supreme Court when the next vacancy arises." American Conservative Union press release (Bill Lauderback), June 23, 2005 (bold in original), https://web.archive.org/web/20060913192249/http://www.conservative.org/pressroom/06232005_un.asp.

13. See Justice John Paul Stevens, "Kelo, Popularity, and Substantive Due Process," Fall 2011 Albritton Lecture, Univ. of Alabama School of Law, November 16, 2011 (available on line).

14. *National Federation of Independent Business v. Sebelius*, 132 S.Ct. 2566 (2012); *King v. Burwell*, 135 S.Ct. 2480 (2015).

15. The problem arose when state governments opposed to Obamacare chose not to set up health exchanges, necessitating federal exchanges. In addition, the language of a part of the thousand-page bill on its face seemed to limit subsidies to policies purchased on state exchanges. In fact, according to insiders, the intention was to exclude private exchanges, not federal ones. And because the Democrats lost their sixty-vote filibuster-proof majority, they could not risk trying to get a revised version of the bill through the Senate. See Robert Pear, "Four Words that Imperil Health Care Law Were All A Mistake, Writers Now Say," *New York Times*, May 2, 2015 online.

16. But cf. Bradley S. Watson, "Reclaiming the Rule of Law after Obergefell," *National Review*, July 9, 2015, and Ryan T. Anderson, *Truth Overruled: The Future of Marriage and Religious Freedom* (Regnery, 2015). The "truth" Anderson refers to in his title is that "the essence of marriage [is] a male-female union" (2).

17. This law was passed after the Supreme Court decided a free exercise case by setting aside the "compelling interest" test, which the Court had previously applied any time an individual objected to a law neutral on its face toward religion but which an individual claimed posed a "substantial burden" to his or her free exercise of religion. The Court rejected Congress's attempt to require the Court to employ this test against state laws. But as an Act of Congress, RFRA has the effect of supporting free exercise claims against any federal law. And 21 states have passed their own religious freedom restoration acts. Cf. Wikipedia. In addition, when a Kentucky clerk refused to issue marriage certificates to same-sex couples, a

compromise was worked out, albeit with the assistance of a federal district court judge. The clerk's signature is no longer necessary for a valid marriage certificate. See www.mcclatchydc.com/news/politics-government/article67889147.html.

18. See *Burwell v. Hobby Lobby Stores, Inc.*, 134 S.Ct. 2751 (2014).

19. But see *Bob Jones University v. United States*, 461 U.S. 574 (1983). The Court might be able to distinguish the *Bob Jones* case from my example of a university's policy on married student housing. In the *Bob Jones* case, the university claimed that its religious beliefs opposed racial integration. The Court upheld the IRS ruling that such discrimination prevented the university from receiving tax-exempt status. It noted that the IRS policy was authorized by Congress and thereby passed strict scrutiny. Since I am assuming that the university would admit a married same-sex couple but simply not offer them university housing, strict scrutiny might well result in support for the university.

20. In two recent cases, state courts have upheld public accommodations laws that prohibit discrimination based on sexual orientation—as applied to religious free exercise claims raised by individuals who offer personal services to the public for a fee but who object to offering their services to same-sex couples for their weddings. *Masterpiece Cakeshop, Ltd. v. Colorado Civil Rights Commission*, CR 2013-0008 (Colo. App., 2015); *Elane Photography, LLC v. Willock*, 309 P. 3d 53 (N.M. 2013), cert. denied, 134 S. Ct. 1787 (2014). Colorado does not have a RFRA, and the state supreme court denied the bakery's petition for certiorari—thereby letting stand the state court of appeals' decision upholding the Colorado Civil Rights Commission's position. Nonetheless, the U.S. Supreme Court granted certiorari in *Masterpiece Cakeshop* on June 26, 2017; according to www.scotusblog.com, both the free exercise of religion claim and the free speech claim will be addressed.

New Mexico does have a RFRA, but there the state supreme court found that the language of the statute clearly limited its application to action by government agencies, and hence did not apply to a suit by a private party:

[T]he statute is violated only if a "government agency" restricts a person's free exercise of religion. Section 28-22-3. A "government agency" includes "the state or any of its political subdivisions, institutions, departments, agencies, commissions, committees, boards, councils, bureaus or authorities." Section 28-22-2(B). The list of government agencies does *not* include the Legislature or the courts. It could be expected that the Legislature would have included itself and the courts in Section 28-

22-2(B) if it meant the NMRFRA to apply in common-law disputes or private enforcement actions. Instead, the examples of government agencies are exclusively administrative or executive entities. 309 P. 3d at 76.

21. For the relevant Senate votes, see *New York Times*, April 6, 2017, when the filibuster was eliminated ("How Senators Voted on the Gorsuch Filibuster and the Nuclear Option"), and April 7, when the 54-to-45 confirmation vote took place ("Neil Gorsuch Confirmed by Senate as Supreme Court Justice").

Acknowledgments

I STARTED WORKING ON THIS SUBJECT AFTER VERMONT'S SUPREME Court decided in 1999 that same-sex couples who desired to marry had a constitutional right under Vermont's Constitution to enjoy the same benefits as opposite sex couples, which left to the legislature the responsibility to choose between extending the state's marriage laws or creating a category of "civil unions." In 2001, I delivered a paper at a conference on "Courts and the Culture Wars"—which was later published in a book by the same name—in which I argued in support of the Vermont Supreme Court's decision requiring equal benefits but leaving the marriage designation to the legislature and the governor. In 2009, Vermont passed a law extending marriage to same-sex couples.

I began teaching a course on the subject of same-sex marriage in 2006, and sometime after that, with the encouragement of my brother, Paul, I contemplated a book-length study, which would focus on the issue of legislative versus judicial decision-making in the context of republican government. Thanks to the invitation of my former student, Marie Horbar, editor-in-chief of the *Vermont Law Review* during the academic year 2013–14, I published a version of my argument just before the U.S. Supreme Court agreed to take up the issue of same-sex marriage (*Vermont Law Review*, vol. 39, no 2, pp. 275–340). I am grateful to Thomas Pangle, Giorgi Areshidze, and James Stoner for inviting me to present my thoughts on same-sex marriage to attentive audiences at the University of Texas at Austin, Claremont McKenna College, and Louisiana State University, respectively. I want to single out three sources of special support and assistance in my thinking about and writing of this book. I benefited tremendously from Eva Brann's comments on my law review article, as well as conversations with her, and her remarks on tolerance in her essay "Mile-High Meditations," published in *Homage to Americans* (Paul Dry Books 2010). My brother, Paul, encouraged me by assuring me that I had an important argument to make, and that it was as much about judicial review and its place in American constitutionalism as it was about the particular issue of same-sex marriage. He has also done his best to get me to write in a clear, straightforward style. And the staff at Paul Dry Books subjected my manuscript to meticulous editing, including John Corenswet's extensive series of questions aimed at forcing me to clarify my meaning. Every time I addressed these questions, I discovered that John had found me out, that what I had written did not say what I meant to say or did not make it clear enough to be readily understood. I have tried to address all his questions; whether or not I have succeeded, the book is much clearer as a result of that "strict scrutiny."

In addition, a number of friends and former students assisted me with research and comments. Rachel Frank and Jeff Hetzel read the entire manuscript; their questions and comments were very helpful. Others read and commented on parts of the manuscript or the law review version of the work and tracked down articles or provided citations for me. They include Stanley Bernstein, Keegan Callanan, Abel Fillion, David Levy, Margaret Moselander, Alyssa O'Gallagher, James Stoner, and Barry Sullivan. I would also like to thank Charles L. Becker, senior managing editor of the *Vermont Law Review* in 2013–14, who provided citations and constructive suggestions.

Finally, I am grateful to the students who took my J Term course on same-sex marriage. Their probing questions, including whether what I attributed to nature was not in fact due to "social construction," helped me to make a fuller argument.

Murray Dry
Middlebury, Vermont
September 2017

Index